LOCOMOTION PAPERS

NORTHERN NORTHUMBERLAND'S MINOR RAILWAYS:

Volume One
Brickworks, Forestry, Contractors, Military Target railways and various other lines

by
Roger Jermy

THE OAKWOOD PRESS

© Oakwood Press & Roger Jermy 2010

British Library Cataloguing in Publication Data
A Record for this book is available from the British Library
ISBN 978 0 85361 703 7

Typeset by Oakwood Graphics.
Repro by PKmediaworks, Cranborne, Dorset.
Printed by Cambrian Printers, Aberystwyth, Ceredigion.

This book is dedicated to my two grandsons, Oliver and Noah

From the same author (all in preparation):

North Northumberland's Minor Railways: Colliery Lines
North Northumberland's Minor Railways: Sandstone, Whinstone and Gravel Lines
North Northumberland's Minor Railways: Limestone Industry Lines

Rear cover: Blue-liveried *Bunty*, Alan Keef 85R/2010, runs along the ledge above the River Till as it approaches the Heatherslaw Light Railway terminus at Ford Forge at the end of its return journey from Etal. *Author*

Published by The Oakwood Press (Usk), P.O. Box 13, Usk, Mon., NP15 1YS.
E-mail: sales@oakwoodpress.co.uk
Website: www.oakwoodpress.co.uk

Contents

	Introduction	5
Chapter One	**Brickworks Tramways**	8
	1 – The Scremerston Brickworks Tramway	10
	2 – The Chatton Brickworks Tramway	11
	3 – The Thrunton Brickworks Railway	13
	4 – The Learchild Tramway	17
	5 – The Shilbottle Brickworks Tramway	18
	6 – The Amble Brickworks Railways	19
Chapter Two	**The Forestry and Timber Railways of World War I**	23
	7 – The Canadian Forestry Corps Railway at Harbottle	24
	8 – The Canadian Forestry Corps Railway at Thrunton	33
	9 – The Canadian Forestry Corps Railways at Chillingham	41
	10 – Colonel Leather's Railway at Middleton Hall, Belford	45
Chapter Three	**The Later Forestry and Timber Railways**	57
	11 – The Swarland Wood Forestry Railway	58
	12 – The Rothley Forestry Railways	59
	13 – The Ewesley Forestry Railway	60
	14 – The Chathill Forestry Railway	61
	15 – The Alnwick Sawmill Railway	63
	16 – The Sanctuary Wood Sawmill Railway at Denwick, near Alnwick	64
Chaper Four	**The Military Target Railways**	65
	17 – The Ross Links Target Railway	65
	18 – The Silloans Target Railway, near Redesdale Camp	69
	19 – The White Spot Target Railway	72
Chapter Five	**The Passenger-carrying Railways near Berwick**	76
	20 – The Spittal Miniature Railway	76
	21 – The Heatherslaw Light Railway	78

Chapter Six   **Contractors' Railways** 84

22 - McKay & Blackstock's Royal Border Bridge

Contractor's Railways 85

23 – Meakin & Dean's Alnwick to Coldstream Branch

Contractor's Railway 87

24 – Sir John Jackson's Seahouses Harbour

Contractor's Railway 89

25 – The Whitaker Brothers Contract for the

North Sunderland Railway 91

26 – The Reservoir Railways at Fontburn 91

Chapter Seven   **A Varied Collection of Other Railways** 99

27 – The Marshall Meadows Seaweed Railway 99

28 – The Dewar's Granary Railway at Berwick-upon-Tweed 103

29 – The Lemmington Hall (Felbridge Monument)

Railway, near Alnwick 107

30 – The Little Mill Preservation Society's Railway 108

Chapter Eight   **Proposed Railways** 109

31 – Sir Francis Blake's Railway 109

32 – The Berwick & Kelso Railway 111

33 – The Flodden to Barmoor Railway 114

34 – The Marquess of Waterford's Railway 115

35 – The Holy Island Branch Railway 117

36 – The Seahouses Miniature Railway................................... 119

37 – The Aln Valley Railway.. 119

38 – The Military Railway at Bellshiel, Otterburn 124

Acknowledgements.. 125

Bibliography 127

Introduction

This short series of books, under the generic title of *Northern Northumberland's Minor Railways*, will consist of four volumes:

North Northumberland's Minor Railways: Brickworks, Forestry, Contractors,
   Military Target railways and various other lines
North Northumberland's Minor Railways: Colliery Lines
North Northumberland's Minor Railways: Sandstone, Whinstone and Gravel Lines
North Northumberland's Minor Railways: Limestone Industry Lines

'Northern Northumberland' is regarded as encompassing that area of the county lying within the administrative districts of Berwick-upon-Tweed and Alnwick. Until the mid-19th century part of the area covered lay within the County of Durham.

The term 'Minor Railways' is used here to include lines variously referred to as railways, tramways, wagonways and craneways, whether of narrow or standard gauge, which were not owned or operated by the 'main line' railway companies. Thus lines, such as the Rothbury branch, or Alnwick to Coldstream branch, do not feature as they were part of the North British Railway (NBR) and North Eastern Railway (NER) respectively. Later both became part of the London & North Eastern Railway (LNER) and British Railways (BR). A decision was made not to include the North Sunderland Railway (NSR) as its history has been fully described elsewhere (*see the Bibliography*). This line, though privately owned, was essentially a branch from a main line and was, for a time, operated by locomotives hired from the LNER. Similarly these books do not cover lines which were essentially worked as sidings from main lines, such as those servicing Easington Quarry at Belford, or the dockside branch railway at Tweedmouth. Finally the decision was taken not to include a treatment of underground railways, or railways that predominantly ran underground, for example that at Elsdon Colliery.

Nevertheless a few liberties have been taken. For example the railway linking the Blaxter Quarry in Redesdale with Knowesgate station has been included even though, soon after leaving the quarry, it departs from the Alnwick District. Similarly this book includes a description of both of the target railways on the Otterburn Training Ranges in Redesdale, even though one of them is located a few hundred metres outside the Alnwick District boundary. However, its inclusion is justified as this railway was first built and operated at Ross Links, on the North Northumberland coast south of Berwick, before being removed to Redesdale.

No attempt has been made to convert former imperial units into the present-day metric form. Units appropriate to the time of each railway have been used. Thus boiler pressures, for example, are referred to in pounds per square inch and costs are described in pounds, shillings and pence where the original source materials used these. Where metric units have appeared in original documents (such as the recent Heatherslaw Light Railway brochure which refers to the line as being 6.4 km in length) they have been retained.

The lines covered in these books were constructed for a wide variety of purposes. Some were associated with the many quarries, whether limestone, whinstone or sandstone, in the area. Others were linked with the coal mining industry. Some served brick and tile works, whilst others were built for military

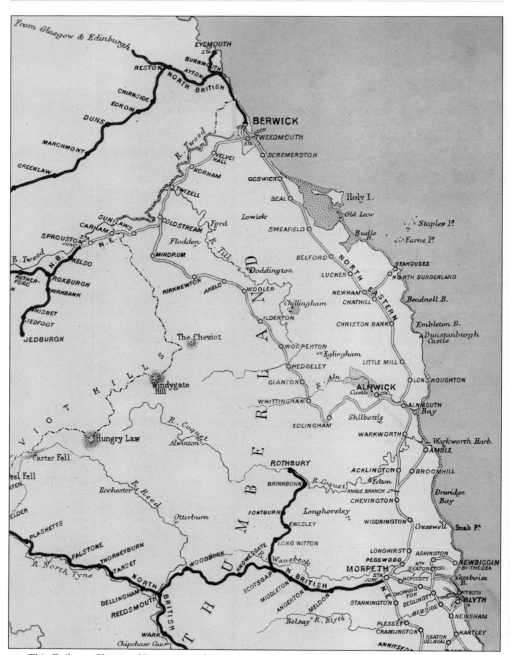

This Railway Clearing House map of 1917 shows the 'major lines' and stations of the northern part of Northumberland. A number of these lines and stations are referred to in the text, as some of the area's minor lines had links with them.

Oakwood Collection

purposes. The forestry and timber industries were responsible for the creation of some lines and in recent years small lines have been constructed for the tourist industry. Almost exactly 200 years of local railway history are covered in these books.

Whilst it has been necessary to include some technical railway details it has also been considered important to place the railways into their social, geographical and historical context. Hopefully this will widen the readership of the books. The purist may consider it an important omission that lists of source materials and references have not been included after each chapter. If readers wish to make an individual study of the sources that have been consulted then they are cordially invited to get in touch with me via the publisher. Whilst researching for the books it has been considered a top priority that original sources be consulted, and that visits be made to as many of the sites as is practicable or possible. Oral ('anecdotal') evidence, and evidence from secondary sources, such as newspaper reports, has been used on various occasions. However, memories, particularly of events that happened nearly a century ago, may have become clouded, and every effort has been made to find written material which corroborates the evidence of the spoken word. On occasions it has been realised that the details reproduced here differ from previously published material. Hopefully, I am correcting earlier errors rather than introducing new ones; nevertheless I accept full responsibility for any mistakes in the text.

At many points in the books I have referred to lines or their remains being on private property. Permission must *always* be sought from landowners or tenants before visits are attempted. In certain cases the sites of railways, or former railways, can pose considerable danger to visitors, for example from steep cliffs, falling rocks, marshy ground or deep water. The surviving military railways pose a particular threat as they are located within still-active training areas where live ammunition is used. Visits to these lines are extremely dangerous if not carefully supervised by appropriate expert personnel. The flying of red flags, the display of red lights and the presence of secure fences indicate danger and the instructions on warning notices must be followed.

These books, whilst attempting to be comprehensive, cannot claim to have included every detail about the railways. Written records of some are sparse or incomplete, and, in the case of many of the lines, there is no one still alive with personal memories to impart. The author would therefore welcome the receipt of any information, perhaps from family histories or albums, which adds to the story of any of the lines. Old photographs or postcards, for which the author has been searching for several years, can provide valuable insight into the working of a line. Some, including those in Archives, Record Office and private collections, have proved impossible to reproduce satisfactorily. However, it would be a pleasure to receive details of any others that have survived.

Roger Jermy
Alnwick
Northumberland
2010

Chapter One

Brickworks Tramways

The north of Northumberland had numerous brick and tile works, very few of which have worked in recent years. Cartographic, and other evidence, suggests that at least six of them employed small tramways or railways. Though there appears to be no evidence from surviving document or maps it is almost certain that some of the other larger works, such as the Ewart Brick and Tileworks, formerly located to the north of Wooler, would have used tramways also. At Ewart, for example, the site was extensive, the clay pits were deep and eventually some way from the works buildings. Manpower, using carts or sledges alone, would have had difficulty supplying the brick sheds. Others would have employed small tramways within their buildings, for example for the movement of unfired bricks to the kilns. Such 'undercover' lines do not appear on maps and are rarely recorded.

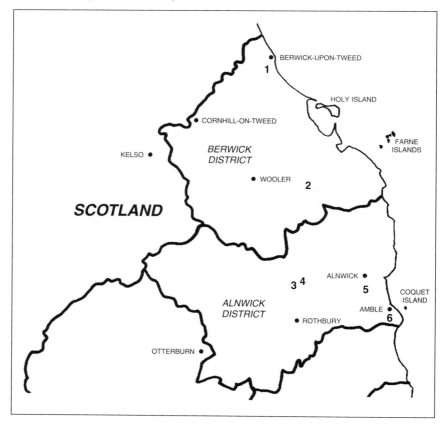

. Brick and tile making requires a source of clay. This is obtained from surface deposits of recent geological origin. Clay is an awkward material to work with. When dry, clay shrinks and becomes very hard. When wet it becomes sticky, and, at a certain water content, it shows 'thixotropic' properties and turns to the consistency, particularly when disturbed by wheels or feet, of a thick 'chocolate sauce'. In very wet conditions it becomes almost impossible to move a cartload, by human or horsepower, across a clay field. In such situations the use of a tramway, laid on sleepers to spread the load and to prevent contact between the wagon wheels and the ground, is a distinct advantage.

To make bricks or tiles the clay has to be dug, either from surface pits or underground. In the 18th and 19th centuries this was done manually, with mechanical diggers not being employed until much later, in the 20th century. When distances were very short the clay was originally shovelled into a small cart, or onto a sled, and taken to the brick and tile sheds. The later use of wagons on tramway rails facilitated this clay movement. At the sheds, clay of the correct mix and consistency was put into wooden moulds. The unfired, or 'green', bricks were then moved, often on more tramway rails, to be placed in a clamp or kiln where they were fired. The loading of unfired or 'green' bricks might take about two days, whilst the 'curing' at a lower temperature, took up to three days. Finally the temperature was raised to 'full heat' (three more days) with a further three to four days 'cooling down time'. The bricks could then be unloaded; once again a tramway could be involved in moving the fired bricks from the kiln. As well as bricks, a brick and tile works would often make roof tiles, ridge tiles, finials, chimneys and drainage pipes whilst some products also involved decorative work.

Records show that there was a huge increase in the number of brick and tile works in the 1850s. In industrial areas this could have been attributed to the construction and expansion of brick-built houses in towns or to the expansion of the coal, iron and steel industries. However, in largely rural areas, such as the north of Northumberland, the increase was largely attributable to developments in agriculture when many pipes were needed to effect land drainage schemes. Former unproductive wetland or moorland was drained and converted into land suitable for grazing sheep. In the 1850s, in the vicinity of the brick and tile works at Shilbottle, for example, some 77 per cent of the Longhoughton acreage was under-drained, and at Shilbottle itself some 69 per cent. In Northumberland as a whole the number of brick and tile works increased from about 12 in 1845 to over 130 in 1865! By 1875, after the completion of drainage schemes on many of the estates, the number fell back to about 80. Many of the remainder would close over the following 50 years. Only a few survive today.

1 – The Scremerston Brickworks Tramway

There are three sites at Scremerston where brick and tileworks formerly operated. The first, which operated in the early to mid-19th century, was close to the cliff top near to the site of what became Sandbanks (or 'Sea Side') Limeworks (NU032482). It was known as the Sea Side Brick & Tile Works. The clay pits were located close to, and to the east of, the works. The works, latterly managed by John Winter, is known to have closed in the mid-1850s.

The second brick and tile works at Scremerston was the Borewell Works which was located on How Moor at the site of the old (1828-1840) Restoration Pit, just to the north of the still-surviving Deputy Row cottages (NU008496). There was a building known as the 'Clay House' and to the north and west were located the clay pits. However, no evidence has been found to confirm that there was a tramway or railway at either of these two locations.

The third brick and tileworks was located on the opposite side of the Great North Road and to the north-west of Borewell. It was known as the Scremerston Tileworks (NU 003498). It was in existence by the time of the first OS maps and pre-dated the Scremerston Colliery which was sunk close by. Records indicate that in 1850 a Mr A. Christison was operating the works, to be replaced by R. Hall & Co. by 1855, and R. Johnson & Co. by 1858. The works made bricks, drain pipes and, later, flower pots of different sizes. Its clay pits, with a depth of 17 ft of clay, were located a little to the north, adjacent to the main road. A narrow gauge tramway or railway, probably with easily-portable rails, was constructed

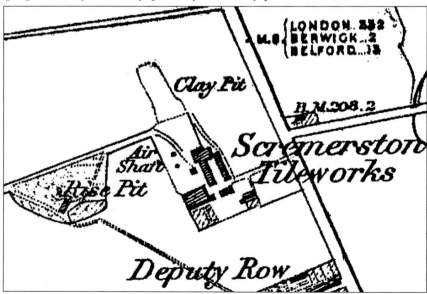

Scremerston Brick & Tile Works is shown on this OS map located about two miles from Berwick by the Great North Road.

Ordnance Survey, Crown Copyright, all rights reserved

to take the hand-cut clay, using, apparently, a single truck from the pit into the brickyard. A Lancashire boiler and engine supplied the works with power. After rain the clay pit was prone to flooding and a small vertical-boilered engine and pump were used to remove the water. What is probably the alignment of the tramway between the pit and brickyard is marked on the First Edition OS map, though it does not appear on subsequent maps.

After the later sinking of the nearby pit, the clay to make the bricks came from a 2½ ft layer of 'seggar' (clay shale) which was found beneath the 'Cooper Eye' coal seam. The brick and tile works then employed a workforce made up of a machine man, a mill man, a mixer, two 'runners' (whose job was to move 'green' bricks using a tramway and set them into the kilns), three burners and two drawers. The brickworks produced bricks which were recognised by the initials 'S M C' moulded into them (Scremerston Main Colliery). Later, a new brickworks operated under the umbrella of the Scremerston and Shoreswood Colliery Company. According to a plan drawn by a Mr T. Brown in 1925, this works had a bank of nine kilns, with one older one nearby. There was also a building labelled 'The Pottery' which was where moulding and decorative work took place. A horse-drawn tramway crossed the A1 road to a clay pit on the opposite side. This works finally closed just before the adjacent colliery at the end of 1943 or start of 1944. The tramway rails and wagons were disposed of and no remains are left at the site.

Whilst most of the Scremerston bricks were used locally, some were 'exported' by rail from the siding at Scremerston station. The NER's returns for the year before the start of World War I indicate that 518 tons left the area this way.

2 – The Chatton Brickworks Tramway

This works has been referred to, at different times, as Chatton Brickworks, Chatton Tileworks, Chatton Brick & Tile Works and Greendykes Brickworks. The brickworks tramway, at Chatton, shown on the OS maps published just before 1900, was a narrow gauge line, running approximately north-south, linking the clay pit and the 'Chatton Tile Works' where the clay was moulded into bricks (NU065285). The works was marked as 'Disused' on this map. It was presumably laid, as in other brick and tile works, with lightweight rails. It consisted, according to map evidence, of a single line with no sidings. Presumably it was a portable line and could be moved or extended to wherever the clay was being dug at any given time.

The site of the 'Chatton Tile Works' (as it is called on OS maps) is to the south of the Belford Road, about one kilometre to the east of Chatton village. Entrance to the site was from the track leading from Chatton to Shielhope Farm. The works, apparently built around 1850, is first referred to in *Whillans Guide* of 1855 which refers to 'R. Hall and Company, Brick and Tile Manufacturers' of Chatton. A cottage, today called 'Tilery Cottage' (the former Manager's cottage), is located at the side of the road adjacent to the former clay field site. A building referred to as the 'Brick shed' survives a short distance to the east of this cottage. By 1866 the 'Chatton Brick and Tile Works' (as it was then called) was in the hands of a contractor called William Guttridge, who had moved from the appropriately named Tileby in Lincolnshire via the tileworks at Long Houghton, where he is recorded as working in 1856. He lived in Old Lyham, then for a time at 'Brick Shades' (perhaps 'Brick Sheds') House, Chatton. He was assisted by his son, James, and perhaps at first by a Thomas Tully, who described himself as a 'Retired Brick and Tile Maker' in the 1881 census. His daughter, Elizabeth, married Adam Hall (or Hale), described as a 'Tilemaker' at Chatton Parish Church on 27th December, 1866. William Guttridge continued to add to his family in the 1880s. Perhaps his first daughter called Elizabeth died because in 1887 another daughter received the same name. William probably gave up tile and brick making around 1890 for by 1892 the tilemaker at Chatton was a certain George Archbold. The works had a single 'Newcastle kiln' measuring 15 ft 6 in. by 13 ft 6 in. by 9 ft 6 in. in height.

By the mid-1890s the OS map records the Chatton Tile Works as being 'disused' though the narrow gauge railway is still shown as being in place. By the next OS maps, produced in the early 1920s, the brick sheds and kiln at the works had been demolished and the tramway had disappeared. No records have survived of the operation of the tramway, its wagons or mode of operation, though in view of its limited length, at most 100 metres, it probably relied on manpower for propulsion of the clay tubs.

This is the site of the former Chatton Brick & Tileworks. The brick shed survives on the right of the photograph and the former Manager's house (formerly 'Brick Shades' or 'Brick Sheds House', now called 'Tilery Cottage') is on the left. The tramway ran to the clay pit in front of the brick shed.   *Author*

3 – The Thrunton Brickworks Railway

Brick and tile manufacture is believed to have commenced at Thrunton in the first part of the 19th century. The original works was situated to the west of the Morpeth to Wooler road (now the A697) a couple of miles north of its intersection with the Alnwick to Rothbury road (now the B6341) at Moor House crossroads (NU092096). The 20th century works was located a short distance further north, though its clay pit extended south and westwards beyond the site of the former works.

An advertisement for 1816 refers to a 'Tile Field' in the area, operated by one George Philips. By 1851 the tile maker at Thrunton was George Sanderson who lived on site at Thrunton. No other local residents were described in the census as being involved with brick or tile manufacture though it is possible that some of the 'labourers' living in the nearby Whittingham Lane may have worked here. Ten years later the business, then referred to as 'Thrunton Tilery', had clearly expanded as three tilemakers lived at Thrunton. George Sanderson, by now 67 years old, was still present but he had been joined by a Scottish tile maker, Hugh Chambers (aged 53), and his son, William. The first OS map shows the Thrunton Tile Works to the south of the village of Thrunton, with its small clay pit on its west side (in the direction of Thrunton Red House). Excess water from the site drained into the nearby Coe Burn. A track linked the works with the nearby Morpeth to Wooler road just south of the Ravensworth Arms public house. The map does not show any existence of an internal railway at this time, the clay presumably being moved to the kilns by cart (in dry conditions) or by sled.

A long wheelbase four-wheeled flat wagon, formerly used for carrying palletted bricks, lies dumped at the Swarland Brick Company. Similar wagons are still in use inside the works building.
Author

This 2009 panoramic view of the Swarland Brick Co.'s works is taken from below Thrunton Woods. The works is to the left and the clay pits, now served by a conveyor rather than a narrow gauge railway, lie to the right. *Author*

This photograph was taken of the locomotive at Swarland Brick Co. works after it had ceased to lead clay from the clay pits. Lister No. L36745 is seen out-of-use amid piles of scrap materials at the works on 27th December, 1967. Behind it and to the left are the remains of several of the flat wagons used for carrying palletted brick loads. *Peter Nicholson*

The census of 1871 revealed that the sole tile maker at 'Thrunton Tile Shades' [sic] was William Chambers, by now aged 29 and married with an Irish wife. Living at his house was a lodger Felix Watson, described as a labourer, who may have assisted at the works. Ten years later they had moved on and the works was operated by a Joseph Thompson, described as a 'brick and tile maker'. The birthplaces of his children would seem to indicate that he moved to Thrunton from Radcliffe, Northumberland, in about 1879. For how long Thompson operated the works is not known but by the date of survey of the 1890s OS maps the works is described as 'disused' and most of the associated buildings appear to have been demolished. Once again the maps give no indication of the existence of a railway, though the increasing distances between the clay pit and the works would have made one very useful. By the 1920s the works was still in disuse and even the nearby pub had been closed and converted into a private house, known as Learchild Moor House.

The 'new' brickworks (NU092098) opened just to the north of the old one. It was established by Commander Vines, RN, who created work for some 35 unemployed men from Tyneside. The works closed in 1939 and the men lost their jobs. However, Chay and Matt Blythe of Birtley bought the works in 1942 and it was reopened under the name of 'The Swarland Brick Company'. It was served by a gravel track, later surfaced with tarmacadam, which branched off from the one leading to the 'old' works. By this time the County Council had widened and improved the Morpeth to Wooler road and this was used for the distribution of the brick and tile products. Some Thrunton bricks are known to have been transported to as far away as Ullapool in north-west Scotland in connection with the building of a tweed mill there.

The buildings at the works were large, and very extensive clay pits were dug out, initially to the west of the works and then to the south. The Swarland Brick Co. built a railway of 2 ft gauge to bring the clay towards the works. The clay was taken to an elevator which led the clay into the top of the pugmill. For the first few years men pushed the tubs but this became impractical as the digging sites became further away from the works. The use of manpower was therefore replaced by the use of small locomotives. Unfortunately no plan of the layout of the system has survived and it has never appeared on OS maps. However, it is known that the lines of rail, forming a 'fan' in the claypit, were moved regularly as the sites of clay excavation changed.

At different times three locomotives were used on this system. The first, a 4-wheeled diesel-mechanical machine was obtained new from Ruston & Hornsby (Works No. RH237880/1946). It operated at Thrunton for several years until it was sold to the Choppington Wirecut Bricks Co.

The second was a 4-wheeled petrol-engined locomotive with mechanical transmission, obtained new from Listers (Works No. L35131/1950). This had a longer life at Thrunton, being finally sold to the Butterley & Blaby Brick Companies Ltd, at Blaby, Leicestershire in late October 1967. The third locomotive was another petrol-engined 4-wheeled Lister machine (L36745/1951), also with mechanical transmission, which was rebuilt with a diesel engine in 1960. It was sold to a concern called Amble Engineering, Amble, Northumberland, in about 1970, apparently for use at a planned pleasure railway on the Northumberland coast. This railway did not get off the ground and the locomotive was sold on to a succession of owners before finding its way across to Northern Ireland. (The Amble Engineering Co. Ltd was dissolved in September 1965; the firm mentioned above was presumably a successor.) None of the locomotives carried names or fleet numbers whilst operating at Thrunton. There was no separate engine shed, the locomotives being stabled overnight under cover in part of the works.

The railway was replaced by a conveyor belt system in the mid-1960s, the track being lifted in June 1967. Until 1971 coal from Shilbottle Colliery was used to fire the kilns but the fuel was then switched to propane gas. Today liquid petroleum gas is used. In the 1980s the equipment at the works was modernized with mechanical shovels being used to load clay into hoppers before crushing and being conveyed to the mill at the main works building. At this time the brickworks was producing about 185,000 bricks per week. Today, some 40 years after rail operations ceased, various piles of wagon wheels, track and rails are littered around the works site. At least one of the clay tippers survives as do several of the flatbed wagons used within the works buildings for moving materials to and from the moulds and kilns. Various lengths of track, one bearing a flatbed Hudson wagon, are still *in situ*. The works continues to manufacture bricks successfully, the bricks being taken from the site by road.

A narrow gauge side-tipping wagon on a Hudson chassis photographed at the Swarland Brick company works some 40 years after it was last used to collect clay.   *Author*

4 – The Learchild Tramway

Documentary or cartographic evidence of this tramway appears to be lacking but various local individuals have reported the existence of a short-lived tramway (in the period between 1884 and 1887) which linked the roadside brick and tile works at Learchild (NU103120), to the east of Jockeyside Bridge on the Alnwick to Whittingham road, with the route of the then under-construction Alnwick to Coldstream branch of the NER. The 350 yard-long Hillhead tunnel (northern entrance at NU106110), between Edlingham and Whittingham stations was a major engineering feature on the branch and required lining with bricks. The contractor, G. Meakin & J.W. Dean of Hampstead, London, made their bricks at a small three-kiln brickworks ('Low Learchild Brickworks') adjacent to the trackbed at the north-western end of the tunnel, using clay dug from some small pits located nearby. It has been suggested that this clay source proved to be insufficient and that additional clay was transported along a temporary tramway from the clay pits which had formerly supplied the Learchild brick and tile works. The Learchild brick and tile works (known locally as 'Learchild Tile Sheds') had operated at the side of the Whittingham road during the middle of the 19th century but had closed by 1881. The former brickmaker's cottage at the site was, by that time, occupied by a postal messenger so it is likely that the site simply acted as a source of clay for the railway bricks. Today the cottage is known as Learchild Cottage.

If the tramway did, indeed, exist then it is likely to have been a lightly-laid narrow gauge line employing horses to pull the wagons to the claypit. Gravity would have assisted the movement of the loaded wagons down to the kilns. No remains of rails or light engineering features have been discovered, though the trackway linking the road near to Learchild Cottage with the former Learchild level crossing and Low Learchild farm may follow part of the route.

Neither of the two recently published books (2007) on the Alnwick & Cornhill Railway makes mention of the contractor's brickworks or the clay pit adjacent to the Hillhead tunnel, though they are clearly marked on the 1890s OS maps. Clearly the research conducted by these authors also failed to find any conclusive evidence of the existence of this possible tramway.

Beside and to the east of Whittingham station, not far from Learchild, there was another small brick and tile works, known as the Bridge of Aln Brickworks after the name of a nearby hostelry, the Bridge of Aln Hotel (NU091122). This works existed from around the early 1890s into the first years of the 20th century. It was a small-scale concern managed by a Mr J. Slater and had a sharply-curved rail connection from the adjacent NER line, until it was removed in July 1915. However, this was operated as a standard gauge siding by the main line railway company and no evidence has been discovered of a narrow gauge line within the works. This siding is shown on contemporary OS maps as joining the branch within the limits of Whittingham station, to the north of the road overbridge.

5 – The Shilbottle Brickworks Tramway

The brickworks railway at Shilbottle Brick & Tile Works (NU175081) was some 130 metres in length. The works, originally known as Hitchcroft Tileworks, was situated at a site adjacent to the Great North Road where it was joined by a road from Shilbottle village.

The railway ran approximately north-south and was located some 30 metres to the east of, and parallel to, the present A1. As at Chatton, it connected the clay pit and the brick sheds and was of narrow gauge. It was likely to have relied on human or possibly horse haulage. Maps show the line as single with no sidings. Again it is likely that the line could have been extended or moved to wherever clay was being dug.

The works was built by the Duke of Northumberland as his Estate Tilery in 1847 at a cost of £1,661. The layer of clay was about 8 ft in thickness. The first OS map of the 1860s shows the brick and tile works but with no railway present, the original clay pit being close to the brick shed near the Shilbottle road. Between 1879 and 1894 the works was operated by Robert Thompson who employed five men. His address is listed in the 1881 census as 'Shilbottle Tile Shader' [sic: this should read 'Tile Sheds']. His employees included his two sons, Robert T. and William, who still lived with him even though William was married with at least four children. Thomas Ward, another employee, was his lodger. The works made a variety of bricks and tiles for use on the Northumberland Estate including pipes and drains. Local Shilbottle coal, which burned at a high temperature and gave out much heat, was used to fire the kilns.

Taken, with permission, from the yard of the Fife Reclamation & Plant Hire Works, this photograph shows the remains of the kilns at Shilbottle Brick & Tile Works. The low lying land between the kilns and the excavator attachments is the site of the former clay pit which the tramway served.

Author

By the 1890s the OS map marked the Shilbottle Brick & Tile Works as 'Disused' though the railway is still shown in place. The 1901 census indicates that no-one at Shilbottle was engaged in the brick and tile industry. None of the persons whose names were associated with the brick and tile works in 1881 still lived in Northumberland in 1901. However, there was a brief period of reopening for records show that in 1902 a certain W. Leath was in charge of the works and a J. Anderson in 1906, the year that the works finally closed.

By the 1920s the brick sheds had been demolished and the rails removed though parts of the 'Newcastle-type' kilns have survived for many more years. One collapsed in the mid-1990s but the remains of the other can still be seen from passing cars on the A1, almost opposite the now-closed Hare Crag amenity site. A plant hire and materials reclamation company now occupies the brickworks site with most of the former clay pit having been filled in. Part of the site has been landscaped with young trees planted.

6 – The Amble Brickworks Railways

When the initial borings took place at Radcliffe Colliery it was discovered that beneath the topsoil there were near-surface layers containing yellow, brown and blue clay, with a total thickness of over 20 ft. (At Hauxley the clay layers were even more pronounced and at Broomhill Colliery even reached 60 ft in thickness!) Other clay layers were found much lower down, some being associated with the Princess coal seam, for example. As at Scremerston in the north of the county, a brickmaking industry thus became associated with coalmining. The brickworks, located close to Amble (originally Warkworth) Harbour (NU266048), was in the hands of the Radcliffe Coal Company from the 1870s until 1900. The Broomhill Collieries Ltd were owners from 1901 until 1947 when the coal industry was nationalized.

Commercial extraction of the clay commenced in the 1870s when some 1,800 tons were removed. In 1873, for example, the eight kilns at the works produced some 40,000 bricks per week. Within a few years the amount of clay used had risen to nearly 4,500 tons annually. Cartographic evidence of the brickworks first appears on Thomas Meik & Sons' *Plan of Warkworth Harbour* dated 1891. It is located to the west of the coal staithes. The works is shown as having rail connections from the Radcliffe Wagonway and the NER, with two sidings entering at the level of the adjacent Coquet Street, and two other sidings at the side of the works at a higher level, having crossed Coquet Street on a bridge. These facilitated the arrival of clay, and coal for firing the kilns, at the works. A jetty is marked at the side of the harbour with a 'Proposed new quay line'. The contemporary OS maps show a similar layout. One siding is shown as entering the works buildings. A short line of unknown gauge is seen leaving the opposite side of the works and terminating at a jetty on the quayside; this is described as being 55 ft in length in 1900. This proximity to the harbour and the ease of transferring the bricks onto vessels meant that the works had a lucrative export trade. Cargoes of bricks left Amble for the Baltic ports, for France and ports in the Mediterranean as well as the south of England.

A team of workmen photographed at the Radcliffe Brickworks at Amble. Some of the men on the right appear to be sitting on the chassis of a small wagon.   *G.D. Moffat Collection*

Photographs of Radcliffe Brickworks at Amble have been difficult to trace. This view is of the brickworks when out of use and partially demolished. Regrettably there are no signs of the brickworks tramway.   *Bartle Oliver*

At the start of the 1890s there had been a slight downturn in production with just 1,165 tons of ordinary bricks being sold, together with 32 tons of firebricks and four tons of fireclay. By 1898, however, an investment was made in the works by the owners, the Broomhill Colliery Co., and new plant was introduced including a clay grinder pan and elevators, a mixer and a brick moulding pressing machine. A pair of new 14 in. inverted vertical engines supplied the power. The kilns, two rows of six, were described as being 'to either side of the main brickworks'. The contemporary *Kelly's Trade Directory* contained the following entry:

> The Broomhill Collieries Limited have railways to the Harbour at Amble, terminating in coal staithes, from which coals and bricks are shipped. Here are the extensive firebrick works of the Broomhill Collieries Limited.

By 1914 the brickworks was employing some 26 men, with the foreman, Robert Ballantyne, being paid £2 per week with his assistant, William Ballantyne, receiving £1 10s. per week. The foreman at the kilns, W. Bradford, received an hourly payment of 4s. whilst other workmen were paid between 1s. 8d. and 4s. 3d. per hour. The working week was 48 hours. Rapid wage inflation occurred just after the end of World War I for, by 1920, the 21 employees were receiving from 4s. 2d. to 11s. 10d. per hour. The jobs at the works, were described (in 1926) as burner, moulder, machineman, kiln foreman, setters (3), drawers (3), millman, wheeling coal [sic], ashman, hopperload [sic] and press lads (6), a staff of 20 excluding William Ballantyne (by now titled 'Manager') and his assistant. There are records of bricks being sent from Amble to Newbiggin, Choppington, Alnwick, Charlton, Chatton, Warkworth, Shilbottle Colliery (in course of construction), North Sunderland, Wooler, Belford, Meldon station (near Morpeth) and Newcastle. By 1928 an average of 40,000 bricks were being made per fortnight in the eight working kilns. Occasionally this rose as high as 90,000 depending on demand. On one occasion a total of 145,000 bricks was dispatched in a single week. In addition to bricks the works also produced pipes, chimney tops and various components for kilns and furnaces: tiles, flues dampers and retort bearers. The products left the works by road, rail and sea.

The OS map of the late 1920s shows a similar rail layout to earlier maps though the short siding from the works to the quayside appears to have been moved towards the east. By then the new Radcliffe Quay had been constructed. A photograph reveals the existence of a narrow gauge line within the works, probably associated with the loading and unloading of the kilns. Men provided the motive power for the small wagons. The total length of the railway system within the works, presumably of all gauges, was described as about ¼ mile in length. By this time the works was still employing 22 men. Over the years the clay continued to be obtained from the shale layers at Broomhill, Hauxley and Newburgh collieries.

At least one railway accident, involving derailment of wagons, is known to have taken place in the standard gauge sidings at the works, though there are no records of deaths or serious injuries.

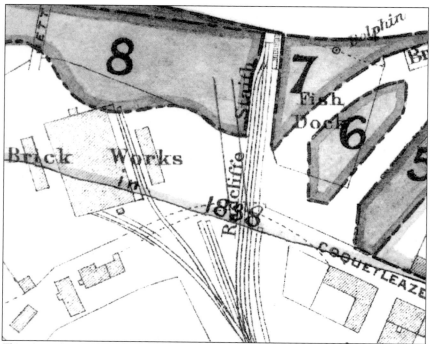

This map, dating from 1891 identifies the original 1838 shoreline at Warkworth, later Amble, harbour. It indicates that the Radcliffe staith, the nearby fish dock and the Amble brickworks and jetty were largely built on land reclaimed from the estuary of the River Coquet. The line linking the works and jetty was not built until later.

Northumberland Record Office

By the mid-1930s a downturn in business had set in and the number of bricks being made was generally down to between 9,000 and 13,000 per fortnight. The locomotives of the Broomhill Co. still shunted the standard gauge brickworks sidings, bringing the wagonloads of clay and removing the empties. Occasionally the company was short of motive power for a report, dated 23rd November, 1938, reads 'No loco available. Hands required to push empty wagon off clay road'. A similar report for 1st January, 1939 reads, 'No clay forward owing to breakdown of loco.'

Brickmaking at Amble continued until final closure of the works in 1958, though the absence of fresh Ordnance surveys at this time meant that the works still appeared on maps published in the 1960s. After closure the brickworks were demolished, all internal and external railway lines and connections were lifted, and the site became part of Harrison's boat building and repair yard.

Bricks made at the Radcliffe Brickworks at Amble bore the name 'Radcliffe' which was moulded onto one side. This brick is now in private ownership.

Author, brick pictured by courtesy of William Stafford

Chapter Two

The Forestry and Timber Railways
of World War I

Before the start of World War I Britain used some 900,000 tons of home-produced timber annually. This compared with the annual 11,500,000 tons which were imported, mainly from Russia, via the Baltic ports, but also from Sweden and Norway. After the start of hostilities these routes became very difficult, if not impossible, as the German fleet controlled the Baltic Sea. However, the need for timber increased greatly as the war progressed. More pit props were required in the collieries as the quantities of coal to service the British fleet soared. Also the military authorities demanded more timber for trenches, telegraph poles, hutted accommodation, ammunition boxes and packing cases. Even the shipyards demanded more timber. At the same time the available manpower for tree-cutting and timber-sawing decreased as more men were called up for military service, particularly abroad.

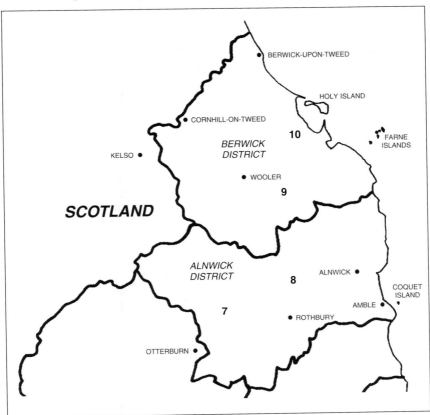

It was thus no surprise when, on 15th February, 1916, as the timber supply crisis increased, that the Colonial Secretary, Mr Bonar Law, made an appeal to the Canadian Government, 'Her Majesty's Government would be grateful if the Canadian Government would assist in the production of timber for War purposes'.

It did not take long for a positive response to be effected and in early May 1916, 1,600 Canadian foresters, belonging to 224th Battalion, arrived in Europe, some being sent to Great Britain and some to France. By the second half of May another 2,000 men, mainly specialist lumbermen, arrived as part of the 238th, 242nd, and 230th Battalions. By the end of the war the total number of men in Forestry Corps service numbered about 17,000! In March 1917 the British Government formed a 'Directorate of Timber Supply' to coordinate and organize the forestry activities and timber distribution. This later became the 'Timber Supply Department', a part of the Board of Trade, and later the 'Timber Disposal Board'. It was wound up in 1922. The Canadian Forestry Corps (CFC) camps in the north-east of England were part of 'District 52' with its headquarters in Carlisle. The men were a mixture of white and native Canadians, Scots (returning home!), Americans and Irish. Assisting at the camps were groups, collectively known as the 'Finns', but really a mixture of Russians, Norwegians, Swedes, Finns, Portuguese and Dutch, together with some interned aliens, and German and Austrian prisoners-of-war. Some of the officers in charge of the camps had been declared 'unfit for combat' as a result of war injuries and thus had been given managerial duties.

A typical camp could include up to 300 officers and men, housed in wooden huts, with stores, a canteen, officers and NCOs messes, a YMCA recreation room, a bath house and showers, medical facilities, workshops and a laundry. Each camp had a flagstaff flying the Canadian flag. The huts were made on site and had a wooden frame, a wood lining covered with tarred paper, and a roof made of timber covered in rubberised felt.

The Canadians brought with them band saws, circular saws, vertical boiler engines and winches, and some traction engines. They erected 'Canadian Mills' which were large (with a 6 ft to 8 ft circular saw) and had 80 hp engines. These required 15 men to operate them. There were also smaller 'Scotch Mills' which were smaller and used 30 hp engines, with only eight men being required for their operation. Jobs included 'fellers', 'swampers' (who cleared branches off felled trees), 'fitters' (who marked the timber for cutting), 'sawyers', and 'haulers', plus the men required to build and operate the camp railways. (Each of the camps in the north of Northumberland operated a rail system.) Finally there were the cooks, administrative and maintenance staff.

7 – The Canadian Forestry Corps Railway at Harbottle

On the 18th May, 1917 the British Government's Director of Timber Supplies, Mr Bampfield Fuller, signed the following document which was sent to the Harbottle Estate in Coquetdale:

In pursuance of the powers conferred upon them by the Defence of the Realm Regulations, the Army Council hereby take possession of the timber (except larch trees and also except specially marked trees in the New Park Wood) belonging to Mr T.C. Fenwick-Clennell of Harbottle Castle, Rothbury, Northumberland, and standing upon the Harbottle Estate in the County of Northumberland .... and to authorise the Officer of the Director of Timber Supplies to do all necessary and proper acts for that purpose. By Order of the Army Council.

However, it was not until the 14th November, 1917 that the advance party of two officers and three other ranks of 115 Company, Canadian Forestry Corps, arrived at Harbottle from their previous camp at Thurstonfield, near Carlisle. They had travelled by train to Rothbury, via Carlisle and Newcastle. Within the next fortnight other parties arrived to start setting up the new camp in a field to the south of Harbottle village, adjacent to the Sharperton and Rothbury road (NT935045). The Unit Diary states:

The new operations of No. 115 Company C.F.C. is [sic] on the Fenwick Clennel Estate [sic] at Harbottle, Northumberland, amongst the Cheviot Hills. The surrounding country is very hilly and consequently the grades are very heavy in places. The nearest Railway Station and shipping point is Rothbury, a distance of nine miles from this Camp.

The shipment of the timber from this railhead was to cause major problems to the unit, not just because of the road distances involved, but also because of the unreliability of some of the vehicles, the lightweight nature of some of the road bridges over local rivers, the generally poor road surfaces and the severely limited siding accommodation at Rothbury station. Also this station's yard was located on the side of a steep hill. Initially the Unit lacked any form of motorized transport, six horses being used to haul the timber, in braked wagons because of the nature of the roads, to Rothbury. The final haul up to the station was particularly difficult!

Serious problems began in December 1917 when there was an acute shortage of suitable vehicles for moving the unit's 'freight' from Rothbury station to the camp site. Although three motor lorries and three petrol tractors had arrived, the only one available for work was one of the lorries! For some days the officials of the North British Railway refused to accept any more freight from Thurstonfield for Rothbury as all of the sidings were occupied by rail wagons awaiting unloading. The problem was solved by a large gang of men being sent to Rothbury with the freight being unloaded onto the platform to await the arrival of more mechanical transport. Eventually the materials (the mill and its building, equipment for the blacksmith's shop, and stores for the quartermaster) were transported to Harbottle and a start was made on camp construction. Typical 'Armstrong' huts (initially 13 in number) were constructed for housing the men, also an orderly room, stores, blacksmith's shop, NCOs mess and officer accommodation.

Timber cutting started on 8th December and by 31st December 4,699 logs (possibly for pit props) and 11,412 linear ft of other timber had been cut, by which time the unit's strength was up to four officers and 147 men. Initially there were just three teams, each of two horses, available. This, initially, limited the overall efficiency of the unit. However, by mid-January 1918 a further 52

This picture, taken from a picture postcard, was taken from the higher land to the south of Harbottle village and shows an early stage in the CFC's timber cutting activities. Some of the camp buildings appear on the right with the huts, and probably the mess buildings, still under construction. *Author's Collection*

Probably taken around the same time as the previous picture this picture postcard view shows the temporary tented accommodation for the men whilst the huts were under construction. The sawmill lies to the right of the centre of the photograph and there is a suggestion of a rail line leading towards it. Both pictures probably date from very early in 1918.   *Author's Collection*

horses had arrived. Of these, 49 were heavy draught horses and three were cobs for the officers. The amount of mechanical transport had also increased, the vehicles on site comprising four motor lorries, two petrol tractors, six trailers, one Ford van, one motor car and one motor cycle. Of these one tractor, three lorries, the car and the motor cycle were 'non-effective'! The number of 'other ranks' had increased, by the end of January, up to 222.

Initially trees were felled in West Wood adjacent to the Alwinton Road (NT 920050) and in the smaller East Wood. The trees were mainly 'Scotch Fir' (Scots Pine), with some poplar, plane and birch. Other trees were cut down closer to the village in the vicinity of the mill which had come into use on 9th January. At first pairs of draught horses were used but two horses could only haul two tons on the level, and the woods around Harbottle were certainly not level.

A decision was made to lay lines of railway to facilitate the movement of the cut trees to the mill. The rails were delivered via Rothbury station and were spiked to sleepers made from tree trunks cut longitudinally and sawn to length. It is believed that lines were laid to each plantation where cutting was taking place. The unit diary recorded:

> The work of cutting and sawing timber in the vicinity of the mill was finished on 20th April and a track was laid to a new cut some distance away. While completing the layout of about half a mile of track, the mill was closed down ...'

One surviving photograph shows the line from the mill forking to head in both westerly and easterly directions. One line certainly reached West Wood traversing the hillside close to 'The Manse' on the Alwinton road. Other lines are believed to have reached New Park Wood, Ramshaugh, Falstone Bank and Camp Knowes woods. All were within a mile of Harbottle sawmill. Whilst horses may have hauled some of the wagons on the lines it is known that use was made of vertical-boilered stationary steam engines, and accompanying winches, to haul the rail wagons by cable. One contemporary postcard, showing such a vertical-boilered engine and winch at Harbottle, has been discovered. Others show the lines in the vicinity of the sawmill and a wagon being unloaded.

Harbottle sawmill, according to the Unit Diary, was engaged in turning the timber into 'slabs, sleepers, boards and posts'. The Alnwick newspaper, which covered the district, recorded: '...the woodcutters... [are]... exceedingly busy, and motor wagons are constantly travelling to and from Harbottle'. Army transport alone could not keep up with the traffic and civilian hauliers, for example, Messrs W. Symington and John Lee of Rothbury, and Selby Morton of Wooler were engaged to assist. From Rothbury station the timber products were sent to a variety of destinations as far north as Dornoch in Scotland and as far south as Kings Lynn.

Some concern was expressed locally about the strength of some of the local road bridges which were crossed by the timber vehicles on their way to Rothbury station. On 3rd December, 1917 the county Surveyor (deputizing for the Rothbury District Council's own Surveyor who was serving with the army in France) reported to the county's Roads & Bridges Committee:

A photographic record of some of the officers and men taken at the entrance to the sawmill at Harbottle. Rails enter the mill in the foreground. The sergeant sitting on the roof joist appears bored by the whole procedure!
Author's Collection

A Holt tractor, fitted with caterpillar tracks, is seen in front of the rail line leading to Harbottle sawmill. This vehicle could haul much larger loads of timber than horse teams but caused much damage to local roads and bridges.
Younger Family Collection

The Canadian Forestry Corps will shortly be loading timber from Harbottle to Rothbury station and they will probably cross three county bridges. At the same time I will make an inspection of the three bridges to see what is the maximum load they are capable of bearing.

The local council approved his intended actions.

The inspection of the bridges was a wise move for the unit took delivery of some new, heavier, Kelly lorries to supplement the five lorries and two tractors (with trailers) that had previously been working, albeit sporadically. The diary recorded that the transport of timber was being hindered by the number of accidents and that consequently some of the vehicles were out of service. In April 1918 it was recorded that of the eight lorries, only three were working. An Austin lorry had not worked at all between January and April and was awaiting repair at a garage in Rothbury. This resulted in an accumulation of timber at the mill. To alleviate the problem a new Holt caterpillar vehicle was brought to Harbottle in June, together with four trailers. It was at this time that the Surveyor inspected the bridge at Sharperton. This was a metal lattice bridge and was already showing signs of damage. The Surveyor imposed a weight limit of three tons on the bridge which meant that the Holt caterpillar tractor could no longer be used over the bridge. Notice of the weight limit was sent to the Local Control Officer, War Office Timber Supplies Department, on 3rd June, 1918. His reply, dated four days later, was to state that road haulage would cease and that an aerial ropeway would be constructed to convey the timber from the woods to Rothbury station! This was not proceeded with and the lighter lorries continued to transport the timber. Another problem then arose. The North British Railway could not ensure a supply of sufficient rail trucks to move the timber from the station. Because the station yard had limited storage it was necessary to hold the timber back at the camp. Fortunately, this situation was not to last for long because in July 1918 orders for timber from the camp were cancelled.

Already a large contingent of 'Finns' had arrived at the camp for the purpose of 'cleaning up the bush'. A gang had been set to work in an attempt to restore and improve the roads between the camp and Rothbury. It was reported that these Finns were 'not subject to military discipline' though incidents, such as those that occurred at Thrunton Camp (q.v.), are not recorded.

In July 1918 the date of 15th August was set for the moving of the men from Harbottle Camp to Appleby in Lincolnshire '...and with this in view the men are doing their level best to get away from here on that date, having had quite sufficient of Harbottle and the vicinity.' The feelings of the men were, perhaps, not surprising for Harbottle was very remote in comparison with some of the locations to which CFC units had been sent. Furthermore their conditions at Harbottle could not have been particularly comfortable. They arrived in November and had to build their own camp in wintry conditions; they did not get electric lighting until March, their unit 'hospital' was not completed until the same month and the first entertainments for the men were not provided until April! Furthermore there had been a severe influenza epidemic which had affected many of the men.

Lengths of sawn timber are being manhandled from flat wagons fitted with four disc wheels. The length of standard gauge track in the foreground appears to have been severed from the line leading into the mill.
Author's Collection

The rail line leads past the hutted accommodation for the foresters. In view are a donkey engine, winch and cables used at Harbottle for hauling heavy loads of timber along the rail lines.
Author's Collection

Loading the Waggons at Harbottle

This picture postcard view was taken to the west of the CFC sawmill at Harbottle. It shows workmen (one identified by hand on the original as a 'Canadian') using an A-frame and ramps to load sawn lengths of tree trunks onto 'waggons' for taking to the mill by rail.   *Author's Collection*

In the event the mill finished cutting on 14th August, 1918 and most of the men left for Appleby on 19th August. Three of the lorries were sent to the CFC unit at Chillingham whilst the others were kept for the removal of the men and equipment. Even then matters conspired against the departing men for the caterpillar tractor, hauling four trailers to Rothbury station, broke down on its journey! The camp was now left entirely in the hands of the Finns who had the job of dismantling the railways, the plant and the camp buildings. Just one officer and three other ranks were left at Harbottle to supervise. Their November diary recorded: 'Everybody is looking forwards towards Christmas'. Not all eventually returned home to Canada; one stayed to marry the lady proprietor of the 'Salmon Inn' at the nearby village of Holystone, one became a local farmer and one became a chauffeur on the Clennell Estate.

The 'Harbottle saga' was not quite over because the lattice-girdered Sharperton bridge had been left in poor condition with distorted girders. The local authority applied to the Timber Supply Department for £3,100 to repair the bridge and a further £32,349 to repair the local roads. When the County Council threatened to close the bridge, the Roads Board Controller offered £500 for the repair of the bridge and then a further sum of £1,000. This was accepted by the council despite their earlier demands! Some timber had remained stockpiled at Harbottle, for, in September 1919, the Timber Supply Department wanted to move 200 tons of it from the site to Rothbury.

One loaded 4-wheeled wagon awaits movement from Thrunton towards the yard at Whittingham. The second wagon, perhaps with two 4-wheeled bogies, is being loaded by the team of foresters. The absence of hills in the background suggests that this photograph was taken close to the wood at Thrunton Mill. *Miller Family Collection*

Three Canadian Foresters pose with a bogie wagon and its load of sawn trunks on the rail line leading from the base of Thrunton Crag to the yard at Whittingham. The chains holding the timber in place and the tools used by the foresters can be seen. *Miller Family Collection*

8 – The Canadian Forestry Corps Railway at Thrunton, near Whittingham

Prior to World War I, only small quantities of timber were produced in the Whittingham area. Some was used locally but small quantities were sent away via the sidings at Whittingham station on the Alnwick to Coldstream branch line. For example in 1913, immediately prior to the outbreak of war, just 511 tons of timber are recorded as having left Whittingham station. This total was to rise dramatically after the arrival of the Canadian Forestry Corps!

It was 112 Company of the CFC that became based at a camp known as 'Thrunton Crag End' (NU073103) located just over half a mile to the south of Whittingham village, north-west of Alnwick. In contrast to the Harbottle camp, that at Thrunton was close to a branch line of a major railway company. Whittingham station (of the NER), sometimes referred to in contemporary documents as 'Whittingham Lane' station, was about a mile away to the north-east of the camp, and as the terrain was relatively flat, it was possible to lay a standard gauge forestry line linking the station with the base of Thrunton Crag. Once again the unit diary survives, as do several photographs taken during the CFC presence at Thrunton. In addition the activities of this unit were better reported in the local newspapers allowing a good picture of the work at Thrunton, Whittingham and nearby Callaly, to be produced.

The first members of the 112 Company, three officers and 76 men, arrived at Whittingham on 19th October, 1916. The men were billeted in a large marquee, but the officers, with Captain Edmunds in command, stayed at the Bridge of Aln Hotel, adjacent to Whittingham station. On the 23rd October they commenced timber cutting at Thrunton Crag and Black Cock Woods, some being used for the construction of their hutted accommodation. The men,

Several wagons, from a variety of main line companies, are loaded with sawn timber in the sidings at Whittingham. The water reservoir for the sawmill's engine can be seen above the wagons. The mill with its tall chimney is to the right behind the stacked logs.

Jimmy Layton Collection

Above: The dumb buffers of the locomotive are clearly seen in this posed photograph of *Imperial*, its driver, and some foresters, taken somewhere on 'the main line' between Thrunton and Whittingham. A timber laden bogie wagon is the first vehicle of the train. Note the deer head 'mascot' attached to the loco's chimney. Its significance is not known.

    Miller Family Collection

Right: The driver of Barclay locomotive *Imperial* No. 238, built in 1881, stands on the footplate in front of the cab during a lull between jobs. A forester appears on the footplate wearing his distinctive uniform hat. The man on the right may well be one of the 'Finns' as his apparel and hat bear no resemblance to a CFC uniform!

    Miller Family Collection

working in teams of two, used the British method for cutting timber, that is, cutting the trunks at ground level rather than leaving large stumps as was Canadian practice. Initially horse-drawn carts and wooden sleds were used to move the cut timber. By the start of December the wooden stable block was built and the mess was almost completed. The machinery for the mill was delivered in the same month as were the first steel rails for the laying of the railway. Five 'cars' were also delivered though whether these were road vehicles or 'flat cars' for transporting timber on the railway is not recorded, probably the latter.

The *Alnwick Guardian* of 11th November, 1916 reported:

> We have at present, staying amongst us in the village of Whittingham, upwards of 80 Canadians, including officers, NCOs and men. They are preparing to hew down timber on Thrunton Crag... a fine bunch of boys...

The officers, with their flat caps and army uniforms, were easily distinguishable from the men who customarily wore uniforms of khaki plus blue overalls and wide-brimmed hats!

The men must have been pleased to move into their camp buildings on 20th January, 1917 for the weather had been very poor, the waterlogged ground having made the movement of timber difficult. However, the arrival of another 150 men enabled two shifts to be worked at the sawmill. At this time a new Commanding Officer, Captain Gillies, took over, with Lieutenants Savoie and Muncaster as his assistant officers. A start was made on laying the railway, 350 feet being laid in January. The locomotive and the timber wagons must have arrived around this time for the unit diary records that on 15th March, 1917, '...the light railway started to bring out the logs cut at Thrunton Crag, but the line was blocked by snow'. However, the locomotive cannot have been in good order as an entry in the diary reads:

> Soon after the loco started running it broke down and had to be sent to Morpeth for a general overhauling, and new bearings were put in throughout. It has since run with very little trouble and has been a great help in saving the hauling of heavy loads over the very poor roads near the camp.

Further construction was taking place at the camp: by April a separate canteen had been created at one end of the mess room, also a reading room. A new bath house was being built and a garage for staff vehicles. By June a YMCA hut had been erected and this was decorated with a Union Flag, a 'God Save the King' poster, and pictures of Canada (including some railway photographs). It was equipped with tables and chairs and a gramophone. A local Whittingham resident, Mr Davies, gave the men regular magic lantern shows here!

The trees near the summit of Thrunton Crag were some 300 ft above the line of railway that was laid in a southwest-northeast alignment along its base. To facilitate movement of the cut timber at least one vertical-boilered stationary steam engine was used to power a winch with 2,000 ft of cable to haul cut logs to the edge of the crag where a 'skidway' or chute was constructed. This allowed the logs to descend towards the railway by gravity. Ramps and A-frames were employed to load the timber onto the wagons for the locomotive to haul them to the sawmill.

Visible evidence suggests that this photograph of the Barclay locomotive with its train was taken at the same time as the one at the top of page 34. The locomotive always faced 'up the gradient' towards Thrunton, presumably to ensure that the firebox crown was always covered with water.
Miller Family Collection

The Canadians enjoyed good relations with the local residents of Thrunton, Callaly and Whittingham. Here, several well-dressed 'locals', accompanied by officers, are seen having a ride up the line on a bogie-wagon with temporary timber-baulk seating. A group of foresters poses on the locomotive footplate on the left.
Miller Family Collection

Just one locomotive is known to have worked on this railway. This was an 0-4-0 saddle tank, built by Andrew Barclay at Kilmarnock (Works No. 238/1881). Whilst at Thrunton it carried the name *Imperial* painted onto its side tanks. It had been supplied new to Lawton & Best for a contract at Paisley, which had finished in 1883. Nothing is known of its subsequent history until it turned up at Thrunton! Its saddle tank was of the 'ogee' form, found on some Barclay locomotives of the 1870s-1880s period. It had a backless cab and was fitted with dumb buffers for propelling the wagons. Whilst at Thrunton it faced westwards, away from the sawmill yard.

The railway, which ran from the base of the Crag, past Thrunton Mill, to the sawmill at Whittingham, was lightly laid, employing 25 lb. rail spiked directly to locally-made timber sleepers. Photographs seem to indicate that there was little or no ballast used. They also reveal that several different types of wagon were used for moving timber on the line; many possessed eight-spoked cast wheels. It is possible that the wagons from the main railway companies were also used on the line. One surviving photograph shows a Great Western Railway wagon and another from the Midland Railway, apparently loaded with pit props. The background suggests that this photograph was taken 'out on the line' rather than at the sawmill sidings.

The sawmill, which was equipped with both a circular saw and band saws, was located in a large field situated between the main Morpeth to Coldstream road (now the A697) and the Alnwick to Cornhill branch of the NER (NU089120). Several sidings were present, both for the timber railway and for 'main line' wagons. An NER map indicates that there was a connection between the sawmill sidings and the branch railway just to the south of bridge 73 at Whittingham station. The connection led to two sidings. One of the sidings was extended by a couple of rail lengths in 1917, to allow the tipping of the accumulated sawdust into a pile. The points for the connection were operated from an adjacent ground frame. On the army land there was a catch point to prevent a train entering onto the branch without proper permission. The frame was 'released' from Whittingham signal box, located to the east of the branch opposite the north end of the station platform. (The later 1920s OS maps show a truncated spur at this point.) Wagons from the Great Central, Midland, North Eastern, Great Northern and Great Western railways all appear in photographs taken at the sawmill sidings or on the timber line.

The unit diary records that the first train load of timber was 'shipped' from Whittingham on 31st March, 1917; it consisted mainly of 'trench sleepers'. The main products of the Whittingham sawmill were such sleepers, 1 in., 2 in. and 3 in. planks and pit props. Other products were telegraph poles and tent poles. Though some of the sawdust was used as stationary engine fuel, the remainder, together with some 'small wood', was dispatched from Whittingham sidings for use as fuel.

On 1st June another 50 men arrived at the camp, mainly axemen and teamsters. On the same day two shifts were introduced on the railway so as to keep the mill supplied with logs. Over the next few weeks further arrivals brought the total strength of the Unit up to 245 all ranks. By this time Lt (Acting Captain) Cameron was the Officer Commanding.

Officers appear to be conducting an inspection at the entrance to the sawmill in the yard at Whittingham. Timber is being unloaded from a rail wagon onto the sawbench.

Jimmy Layton Collection

This photograph shows the 'down side' of the sawmill. A team of horses can be seen on the right-hand side, whilst the sidings contain a variety of wagons from the 'main line' companies, ready for loading with pit props and other mill products.   *Jimmy Layton Collection*

By 4th August the *Guardian and County Advertiser* was reporting:

WHITTINGHAM. The lumbering activities on Thrunton Crag are well nigh on completion. The Canadians are at present engaged clearing Thrunton Mill cover, the trees being about all felled and conveyed to the sawmill. Operations in clearing Whittingham Wood have now commenced. We understand that the timber is to be drawn to a suitable spot for loading by donkey engine and cable. The donkey engine has been used for the same purpose at Thrunton Crag. On Monday the engine was conveyed on the local C.P. railway to near Whittingham Lane [sic] station when it was then drawn on a lumber wagon through the village to the south side of Whittingham Wood. The Canadians have quite a novel mode in moving such a heavy and ungainly cargo as the donkey engine proved to be. Horse flesh was used to steady and keep the wagon on the road, the engine pulling itself by means of the cable being fastened to suitable trees en route to its destination. Those who had the opportunity of seeing them were greatly interested in the methods of the Canadians.

(The reference to the 'C.P. railway' presumably refers to the forestry line from Thrunton; this would have been the easiest way to move the vertical-boilered donkey engine to a surfaced road. Whittingham Wood is located to the south west of the village at NU060114.)

The quantity of timber products ultimately produced at the mill was the second-highest total for any mill in Area 52. On 15th September, 1917 the mill produced 55,400 linear ft of timber in one 10 hour shift! This was a record not to be surpassed at any other camp sawmill in England or Scotland.

With the transfer of cutting from Thrunton to Whittingham Wood and Callaly there was a need for a means of transport of the cut timber from these sites. As an alternative to the movement of the railway to a new alignment some AEC lorries were obtained and these hauled timber to the mill along the public roads. Having caused some damage to the road surface they were also employed in hauling loads of gravel from the river at Hedgeley for road repairs!

By November 1917 the work for the unit in the area began to decline. That month some of the men were moved to a new site close to Chillingham village. Some of the huts were taken down and moved to Chillingham with the men. The *Guardian and County Advertiser* of 15th December reported:

The Canadians in our midst are well nigh finished with the cutting up of the large timber. There still remains a great quantity of small logs to be used for pit props etc. It is understood that about 50 Fins [sic] are to land and encamp at Thrunton Crag End. This batch of men will be clearing up what the Canadians have left in the various plantations.

It was on the day that this article was published that the mill shut down and the work of removing it to Chillingham began. The Finns were to remain at the camp for several months more. One unpleasant incident, which was reported during the Finns' occupation of the camp, was on 15th June, 1918 when some of the Russian Finns indulged in a fight in which razors were used. The affair, witnessed by some of the Swedish Finns was dealt with in a civilian, rather than a military, court.

The railway continued to operate for some time after the bulk of the unit had moved to Chillingham. As late as May 1919 there was a delivery of spares to Whittingham station for the locomotive. These were addressed to the 'Board of

Trade Timber Supplies Department'. The precise closure date for the railway is not recorded. However the Barclay locomotive, No. 238, was auctioned by Robert Handley on 28th/29th April, 1920 as part of surplus sawmilling plant, but it remained unsold. (In error it was referred to as a 4 ft 2½ in. gauge locomotive which may have put off several possible buyers!) Some of the 25 lb. rail and sleepers were in the same sale. By December the locomotive was present in Bott's Jane Pit Storeyard at Walker on Tyneside, where it featured in R. & W. Mack's auction on 21st December, 1920. It was, apparently, sold or scrapped by 30th April, 1921.

In contrast to their colleagues at Harbottle, the Canadians at Thrunton can be said to have had a more pleasurable existence, even working a half-day on Saturdays! The villagers, particularly the young ladies, appear to have welcomed them into their midst! There are several newspaper reports of 'entertainments' being arranged. For example In July 1917 the men were taken to Chillingham where they had '…a rollicking time…visiting sights in the District including the Chillingham cattle'. The same month their football team was beaten 1-0 by a local eleven. In August 1917 they were invited for tea at Callaly Castle. In September they were entertained to a party by the ladies of Whittingham, and in November there was a concert and dance in the rifle range at Whittingham village. In December a shooting competition was arranged. Five of the Canadians married local English girls whilst based at Thrunton, some taking their brides with them to Canada when they returned home. Three more from the unit married whilst at Chillingham. Some settled locally where several babies were born before the end of 1919.

Captain Cameron and Lt McLaren pose next to piles of tree trunks near to the sawmill. Captain Cameron was to find a bride whilst resident at Whittingham. They made their home in Canada after the end of the war.   *Miller Family Collection*

9 – The Canadian Forestry Corps Railways at Chillingham

The official date for 112 Company CFC to arrive at Chillingham, from Thrunton Crag Camp, was 19th October, 1917. In practice the first men arrived on 5th November and immediately began to construct a kitchen and the first building for the camp which was to be known as 'Amerside Law Camp' after the name of the nearby farm (NU062273). The camp, located on the Tankerville's Chillingham Estate, was located about ¾ mile from the village of Chillingham in a field of 30 acres known later as the 'Camps'. After the end of the war, and into the 1930s, some local residents, including Anthony Murray who farmed at Amerside Law, can remember the remains of the huts, particularly bases of the brick-built chimney stacks and an oven, in fields to the north of Oak Wood (NU066271) on the side of Ewe Hill close to the Spindle Burn. In a neighbouring field were two buildings built to house the horses used in the timber-felling operations (in the 1930s they were used as cattle sheds). The trees available for felling were mainly Scots Pine and other softwoods. The nearest railheads were Ilderton (4½ miles away on the Alnwick to Cornhill branch of the NER) and Belford (8 miles distant on the NER's Newcastle to Berwick main line). Both had loading banks and siding accommodation.

The unit diary records that the foundations for the sawmill were started on the 19th November and shortly afterwards the camp boasted four huts for the men, a kitchen-canteen, a mess room, a blacksmith's shop and stable. The sergeants' mess was still under construction. By April 1918 the camp and mill were almost complete: a hospital, wash house, bath house and feed store for the horses had been erected. It was planned to move the YMCA building, erected at Thrunton, to Chillingham. In the event it continued to cater for the needs of the 'Finns' at Thrunton and didn't arrive at Chillingham until June 1918. Rations for the camp were delivered from Ilderton station. The transport available for use of the unit was, according to the Diary, the four 3-ton AEC motor lorries (previously used at Whittingham and Callaly), four general service wagons and a variety of lumber wagons. In addition there were 55 draft horses plus two saddle horses for the officers.

On the 21st November the first consignment of steel rails arrived, after delivery by train to Ilderton, for the construction of the forestry railways. These were to be used to build the line which would serve the Stoneclose and Amersidelaw Hill plantations on the slopes of Key Hill (sometimes 'Kay Hill'). This hill was described in the unit diary as being a crag much like that deforested at Thrunton. Unfortunately no detailed records of this line survive and its 'diagonal' route up the hillside has not been confirmed, though it linked the hill with 'New Drive' where the first sawmill was located. It was certainly steeply graded for Anthony Murray recalled the surviving remains of a timber wagon at the bottom of the hill in the 1930s or early 1940s, reputedly smashed after it had descended the gradient out of control. The only written descriptions of the route are the following which appeared in the Unit Diaries for early 1918:

It is hoped that the light railway will be ready for use early in March and this will reduce the amount of hauling by the logging trucks to the nearest loading point on the road and leave the trucks free to haul lumber to the station.

A slightly later diary entry, when some of the men were still at Whittingham, appeared as follows:

HISTORICAL DIARY NO. 112 COMPANY (cont'd).   52 District

The average strength of men for the month has been 177 with 13 attached from other units, and out of these there havebeen 27 on an average at Whittingham, also 43 Finns. The horses number 53 H.D.

The light railway runs fromthe bush to the mill, and there is also a line running from the mill yard to the road, a distance of ¾ mile. This is stillin course of construction, and will be finished in the following month.

This extract is from the camp diary for 112 Company for April 1918 and refers to the completion of the railway at Chillingham.   *National Archives of Canada*

The known position of the camp and mill, and the references to '¾ mile' and 'the loading point on the road' suggest strongly that the second part of the line followed what is today an east-west track meeting the Chillingham to Chatton road at NU056268. The route of the line 'from the bush' was no doubt altered as the location of tree-cutting changed. There are numerous tracks in the nearby woods which could have been the temporary alignment of rails. The one photograph of the mill which has been discovered does not allow the gauge of the line to be confirmed. There are no records of any locomotive at Chillingham and it is likely that a combination of horses, gravity and vertical-boilered 'donkey engines' with winches were the 'motive power'.

Later in April 1918 the same diary recorded:

The light railway has been of great value in bringing timber to the shipping point on the road ... shipments have been held up for lack of railway trucks and also owing to the fact that only three lorries have been working at the same time all month.

The number of available road lorries for movement of the timber to the local stations (for onward passage to recorded destinations such as Newport, South Wales, and Blyth) was a constant source of concern. At the start of 1918 only six loads of timber were being sent to Ilderton or Belford each day, one of the lorries having to make journeys to Belford to collect gravel to repair the local roads which were being cut up very badly by the lorries. The state of the roads was a source of much concern to the Northumberland County Council. Their Roads & Bridges Committee Minutes, dated 25th March, 1918, contain the following:

The Timber Supplies Department of the Government are carting timber from Chillingham Castle to Ilderton station and they have requested me [i.e. the Surveyor] to send them an estimate of the cost of keeping about two miles of main road in repair during such carting. I estimate the sum of £900 will be required ... Northumberland Whinstone have applied to increase the price of stone to 1/- per ton.

Some gravel was also used on the tracks in the woods before the railway was fully operational. In January one lorry arrived back from repairs at Morpeth but was declared still unserviceable. In March only two of the four lorries were serviceable with the others needing repairs. April was a little better with three of the four lorries available for work but then in May only one was available! To help alleviate the problem an additional 15 more horses arrived from Whittingham, leaving just 15 still there to aid the clearing-up work being performed by the Finns.

By the start of May 1918 most of the timber had been cut in the area near to the mill which was finally closed on 9th May. Timber cutting was moved to a new site at Trickley Wood (NU025270), some two miles to the west of Chillingham, though shipping of stockpiled wood continued from Chillingham. Many of the men were transported by lorry, at the start and end of their shifts, from Amersidelaw Camp (often spelt as three words in the diaries: Amerside Law Camp) to their workplace. The new small camp at Trickley was constructed quickly and eventually consisted of a mill (measuring 85 ft x 30 ft with a concrete base for the engine), stabling for 30 horses, three Armstrong huts (two laid together to form a mess room and one forming a sleeping hut for the millwrights, the filer, the watchman and fireman) and a tool house. The nearest drinking water supply was from the local farm (presumably Fowberry Mains, NU032280) which was nearly ¾ mile away. The mill was about the same distance from Ilderton and Belford stations as that at Chillingham.

The wood at Trickley contained enough trees (mainly hardwood) for only about three weeks' cutting. However, a donkey engine and winch were moved from Chillingham to Trickley to aid the work. The *Berwick Advertiser* of 28th June, 1918 included the following in an article headed 'Canadian Lumbermen':

…when the tree has been felled it is trimmed of its branches and hauled by an endless wire rope from a stationary engine across the low-lying ground to the spot where a light railway has been laid. It is then put on the small trucks and conveyed to the sawmills [sic] about a mile away when it is run alongside a platform on a level with the trucks. The platform holds about a dozen trees.

In view of the length of this line it is possible that the donkey engine and winch, or perhaps horse haulage were used to move the wagons. During July timber operations switched from Trickley Wood to 'Fowberry Wood'. Unfortunately maps fail to reveal a contemporary plantation with this name though Fowberry Park was just to the north of Trickley Wood. A new mill here commenced work on 19th July but operated only briefly, work being completed at Fowberry by August. Two new four-wheel drive vehicles arrived at this time and may have moved the timber from Fowberry.

During August 1918 the mill was moved to a new site in a field at Welsh Mires, to the south of Chillingham Castle adjacent to the Old Bewick to Chillingham road. The mill at this site was referred to as the 'Hepburn Bell Mill'. Tree cutting commenced in 'Welsh Mires' (NU057250), 'Labour in Vain' (NU055251) and 'Oak Wood' (near the former mill site). The mill was ready for work on 22nd August, sawing commencing on 26th. The unit diary records that lumber was placed on '… hand cars coming from the mill … running on three parallel tracks and ... [they] ... can be run to any part of the yard quite easily'. This indicates the existence of a third railway 'system' in the Chillingham area. By September most of the timber activities were taking place at Welsh Mires but with some timber being hauled to the mill from Church Wood. The loading of logs onto the road vehicles had been mechanized with a 'jammer' replacing the former practice of rolling the logs. However, the start of October brought much heavy rain and the roads once again became almost impassable. Two lorries, and the Ford van used for carrying supplies, were at Gosforth for repair. The diary recorded that, 'The 4½ mile haul to Ilderton is difficult'.

In November 1918 the mill was closed for the whole month and a decision was made, as the war had just ended, that the unit would not go to a fresh operation (after having been told that a move to Felton, south of Alnwick, was planned). Accumulated timber was still being shipped from 'Pit Wood'. By January 1919 the number of 'other ranks' in the unit at Chillingham had been reduced to just 118 from a total of 169 a year earlier. Most of these 'surplus' men had returned home to Canada. Work consisted mainly of crating up the mill machinery ready for shipment, and cleaning up the site. The January diary refers to '...a good deal of work ... [having] ... been done on the railway'; this may refer to the track-lifting process. The February diary referred to the continuing bad state of the roads and contained the following:

> The transport has been one of our chief difficulties, which bears out the good sense and judgement in building the mill at Whittingham right on the railway, which does away with the handling of sawn timber etc ... the Board of Trade will soon take over the operation, and leave us free to return to civil life.

This is the only photograph that has been discovered of the Canadian Forestry Corps' sawmill at Chillingham. A laden wagon appears on the rail line at the mill entrance. The officers on the right appear to include Captain Cameron and Lt McLaren.

Author's Collection

The *Alnwick Guardian* of 3rd May, 1919 reported:

The last batch of the CFC left Chillingham on Thursday, 1st May, for their base at Sunningdale, previous to leaving for home. The company of about 30, accompanied by Major and Mrs Cameron, and Lt. Johnson left by the 5 pm train from Wooler station where a large number of inhabitants gave a hearty send-off. Parcels of chocolate and cigarettes were given to the men who cheered the inhabitants before leaving.

(The 5 pm train was the stopping train heading for Alnwick with onward connections, via Alnmouth, to the south.)

On 21st June, 1920 a sale at Chillingham, advertised in the *Timber Trades Journal*, included two miles of railway track. The large piles of timber stored at 'Hepburn Bell Dump' were purchased by the shipbuilders, Alexander Stephen & Sons Ltd, of Glasgow. The Earl of Tankerville, owner of the Chillingham Estate, made a claim for damages due to the operations of the Canadian Forestry Corps and a payments were sanctioned by the Treasury in December 1920 and June 1922.

The social life of the Canadian's at Chillingham did not, perhaps, match that which they had enjoyed at Thrunton and Whittingham. However, some events were held for them including whist drives. The Commanding Officer, by now, Major J. D. Cameron, married Margaret Smith (of Seaton Delaval) at Chillingham parish church and another wedding involving a Canadian took place at nearby Chatton, in addition to the three which took place at Whittingham church whilst the men resided at Chillingham.

A little evidence remains of the Canadians' presence in the Chillingham area. At Chatton a wooden shed building removed from the camp after it closed, still survives behind the Post Office. At Chillingham the remains of some sawpits can still be traced and some bricks at the edge of a field near the camp site at Amerside Law are likely to be the remains of the chimney stacks of the huts. The remains of the steel and wood chassis of two of the timber wagons which rested at the side of 'Bottom Deer Park' field (adjacent to 'The Camps') in the 1930s have long since disappeared. At a roadside location near Trickley Wood, a gravelled area may be the site of the later sawmill and shipment point. Of the three railways there is no evidence, even on aerial photographs.

10 – Colonel Leather's Railway at Middleton Hall, Belford

This 2 ft gauge forestry railway at Belford was an unusual one. Whilst it was primarily constructed for the movement of timber on the Middleton Hall Estate, between the end of World War I and the 1940s it was also used occasionally for the transport of stone, for transporting parties of visitors to view the forestry activities, for transporting forestry workmen and for the transport of shooting parties ('beaters' and 'guns')! Some 'family background' may help explain some of the line's peculiarities and eccentricities.

It was John Towlerton Leather who created the first forestry plantations at Middleton Hall, Belford. Born in Liverpool in 1804, John Leather became a Civil Engineer, contractor (for railways and sea defences) and colliery Manager. He

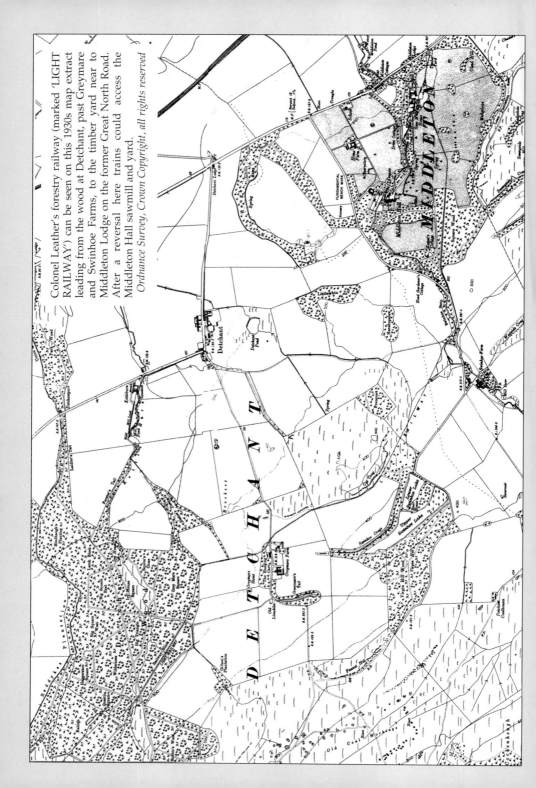

Colonel Leather's forestry railway (marked 'LIGHT RAILWAY') can be seen on this 1930s map extract leading from the wood at Detchant, past Greymare and Swinhoe Farms, to the timber yard near to Middleton Lodge on the former Great North Road. After a reversal here trains could access the Middleton Hall sawmill and yard.

had specialized as a hydraulic engineer. He was also one of the founders of the Hunslet Engine Co. of Leeds. He lived at Leventhorpe Hall in Yorkshire before, additionally, purchasing the Middleton Estate in 1877.

It was John Towlerton Leather's son, Gerard Frederick Towlerton Leather, who, in 1890, inherited the estate after the death of his father. He was born in 1865 and attended Rugby school as a boarder. Forestry was his childhood hobby and he had enjoyed learning the names of trees from his grandfather! After leaving school he served in the county militia and was then commissioned into the Northumberland Fusiliers. His brief military career involved service in the Mediterranean area. His heart was not set on a military career and he retired early from military service to return home (in 1903) to manage the family estates in Yorkshire and Northumberland. Despite having terminated his army career, Leather always retained the title of 'Colonel'.

Colonel Leather developed and improved the forestry activities at Middleton, producing a model estate which involved the creation of a tree nursery, plantations, thinning, felling and subsequent processing of the cut timber. Tens of thousands of trees were planted on the Estate. Leather introduced a water turbine for generating power from electricity. Six small lakes were created to provide the necessary head of water and also to act as a water supply in case of fire. The electricity was used both at the sawmill and in the nearby Hall (as at Lord Armstrong's house at Cragside, Rothbury). He expanded the estate's sawmill and woodworking machinery, built a plant for producing 'suction gas' from sawdust and timber waste, and also a pressure-creosote plant for treating the sawn timber. Later he built his timber-carrying railway. He became one of the advocates of the 'replant after you fell' practice, being described by the *Newcastle Journal* as …'the man who kept on planting trees'. He also officiated at tree-felling competitions!

Colonel Leather's railway did not make an appearance until around the time of the end of World War I in 1918. The first part to be constructed was the section in the vicinity of the yard and sawmill. By 1921 the line had been extended to its north-westerly terminus in the plantations at Detchant Wood. It was laid to 2 ft gauge with rails spiked to wooden sleepers. These sleepers were made from creosoted wood produced on the estate. Unusually the sleepers were made from a variety of woods: oak, ash, beech, poplar, sycamore, elm (both 'wych' and 'English' varieties), wild cherry, and Spanish chestnut! This was part of an experiment conducted by Leather to determine which, in the long run, would be the most long-lasting in normal use. In the event he concluded the trial in 1933 when he discovered that the only sleepers needing replacement were those made from wych elm, English elm, sycamore and 'sapwood-containing oak'. The others were considered to be 'as good as they day they were laid'.

The ultimate length of the line was about three miles. Its extremity was near an area of trees known as 'Quarry Square' in Detchant Wood (NU070370). It passed 'Railway Square' and 'Grey Mare Square' before following the edge of the wood known as the 'Hanging Carr' at Greymare Farm. Crossing two fields below Cat Crag it passed through and then alongside a further plantation, before crossing the fields of Swinhoe Farm. After entering 'Swinhoe Strip' it crossed the Swinhoe Burn on a small, yet substantially-built bridge, before crossing Swinhoe Lane and passing along its south side on a verge. It entered 'Square Wood' before crossing

Above: Two wooden-sided wagons with a load of freshly-sawn timber stand on the line leading from the sawmill in the yard at Middleton Hall.

Above right: Lengths of tree trunk for the sawmill were unloaded from the rail wagons onto a sloping lineside bank near to where the line leading from the timber yard approached the bridge over the burn. Guide rails allowed the trunks to be directed towards the saw bench.

Right: This is a view of the inside of the Middleton Hall sawmill with the saw bench on the right-hand side. The siding from the yard entered into the sawmill building to facilitate the loading of sawn timber into wagons. Its track was inlaid into the mill's floor.

(All) Middleton Hall estate, courtesy of James Boulton, Smiths Gore

Above: The driver of No. LR2795, built at Bedford by the Motor Rail Co. (Works No. MR 1074), propels a flat wagon in the yard at Middleton Hall. Though built for the War Department Light Railway this machine was probably completed too late for it to have been shipped to France for active service there.

Middleton Hall Estate, courtesy of James Boulton, Smiths Gore

Right: This shed was the overnight stabling point for locomotives at Middleton Hall. Here MR 1074 shelters whilst attached to a handbrake-fitted flat wagon.

Middleton Hall Estate, courtesy of James Boulton, Smiths Gore

This is a general view of the yard at Middleton Hall. On the right is the ramp for loading the sawn trunks from rail wagons prior to entry to the sawmill. On the left are several types of wagon for transporting sawn timber.

Middleton Hall Estate, courtesy of James Boulton, Smiths Gore.

The second locomotive used at Middleton Hall was RH 175133 which is seen in 1938 hauling a train of visitors to the estate who were all members of the Royal Forestry Society. Some of the timber wagons have been fitted with temporary seats for the occasion.

Ruston Archive courtesy of Ray Hooley

three fields as it headed towards the Great North Road. From this point the track reversed down the flank of the hill towards the yard where there was a ramp for unloading logs for the sawmill (NU104350). It then crossed the burn on a small bridge, finally entering the yard where there were several sidings, one line serving the mill. Leather reported that it had cost £1,700 per mile to construct.

One of the unusual features of the line was its 'Canadian Pattern' gates at field boundaries which allowed the passage of trains along the line through the fields but prevented the egress of cattle. Each 'gate' was a diamond shaped area, 10 ft wide, fenced around but with openings at each end. The track was laid through this area which was lined with feather-edged planks laid with their thin edge facing upwards; the planks were about four inches apart. The structures functioned in much the same way as the metal cattle grids now employed on some rural roads. It is known that some of the members of the Canadian Forestry Corps remained in Northumberland after demobilization at the end of the war and is possible that they obtained employment at Middleton and provided the knowledge for the 'Canadian Gates'.

Leather is known to have designed wooden bridges for use on light forestry railways and trackways, publishing plans for their construction in the *Journal of the Royal English Forestry Society*. It is possible that such bridges, made from larch, could have been used on the upper reaches of the Middleton line, though the bridge at Swinhoe Burn was of much more substantial construction, with masonry abutments, longitudinal baulks of timber and metal girders providing a firm base for the laying of the rails on the transverse timber sleepers.

So as to cross the public road at Swinhoe Lane it was necessary for Leather to apply for permission from Belford Rural District Council (RDC). The Agreement between Leather and the Council was drawn up by the solicitors, Messrs Adam Douglas, of Alnwick, and was dated 23rd June, 1920.

It read as follows:

> This Agreement permits rails to be laid across the highway, between Middleton Road and Swinhoe Farm, sending along such rails, wagons containing timber and stone, such wagons to be propelled by mechanical power.
> The Owner may lay rails on the grass margin near the fence, four feet from the metalled road, across the road (the road being made good after the rails are laid), gates to be provided at two locations, these to be erected and maintained, steps taken to reduce risk of injury (a light to be shown 1 hour after sunset and 1 hour before sunrise on vehicles, visible in each direction), to indemnify the Council against claims, to remove the rails if the terms were broken, an annual fee of £1 to be paid on the 1st July, all legal expenses to be met by Colonel Leather.

The accompanying plan referred to the line as a 'Tramline' *(see below)*.

There was little doubt that this agreement would have been satisfactory to both parties as Leather had been a member of the RDC since 1913!

The first locomotive purchased for use at Middleton Hall was former War Department Light Railway No. 2795. It had been ordered for service in France during the war but, in view of its dispatch date of 12th November, 1918 it is unlikely to have crossed the channel and seen any hostilities. It was a 20 hp 4-wheeled 'Simplex' petrol-mechanical machine built by Motor Rail of Bedford (Works No.

Above: The Leather family archives contain this delightful photograph of a locomotive breakdown on the Middleton Hall Railway. Judging by the presence of a wind-up gramophone this was taken on the day of a family 'social outing'!
    Leather Family Archive, courtesy of Michael Greene

Right: In 2010 tracks and other remains are still visible in the yard at Middleton Hall. The line curving to the right led wagons towards the sawmill but the purpose of the other line, heading for the small wood is not known; perhaps it was for wagon holding purposes.   *Author*

MR1074/1918). Such locomotives had two forward and two reverse gears and could haul loads of between 10 and 15 tons at 5 miles per hour. A brake wheel and sandboxes were fitted. The last driver of the locomotive, forester Charlie Hall, is known to have carried a very large box of extra sand on the footplate, partly to replenish the sandboxes and partly to provide extra weight for adhesion on wet days!

A delivery of Motor Rail spares to the Middleton Estate dated 7th April, 1920 suggests strongly that the locomotive had arrived by that time. It is known to have worked at Middleton for some 15 years until 1935, though its subsequent fate is not known. It may have been sold for further use or scrapped.

In the very earliest days of the line horses were used to haul the timber. One horse team could make just three return trips per day. The introduction of the Simplex locomotive enabled 11 return trips to be made, thus saving much time in transferring the felled timber from the plantations to the sawbench. The benefits of locomotive haulage were experienced particularly in inclement weather, though the locomotive itself provided scant protection for its driver!

Records show that a second locomotive, this time purchased brand new, was supplied to Middleton Hall. It was obtained to replace the Simplex which was presumably becoming unreliable. The locomotive was a four-wheeled diesel-mechanical machine built by Ruston's (Works No. RH175133/1935). Its axle load was slightly greater than the Simplex, its total weight being 2¾ tons in working order. It was fitted with an 18/21 hp Lister engine (CS 15017). It was dispatched directly from Ruston's to Middleton on 11th July, 1935, working on Colonel Leather's railway until towards the end of World War II. At this time it is believed to have been sold to a timber merchant in Yorkshire for further use.

Photographs show that at least two types of 4-wheeled wagon were used on the line for carrying timber. Some were short with vertical log-rails and hand brakes; others were longer and fitted with sides for carrying planks of sawn timber.

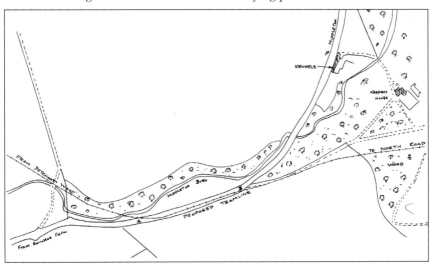

Swinhoe Lane level crossing.   *Berwick-upon-Tweed Record Office*

Right: One surviving point lever remains in the yard at Middleton Hall bearing the name of the German firm of Orenstein & Koppel. This may have found its way to Northumberland after use on a military trench railway in World War I.   *Author*

Below: Some considerable vandalism took place at the site of the former bridge over Swinhoe Brook in 2009. For many years the bridge had been hidden from view by a dense wood, clearance of which laid the area open to vandals.   *Author*

The remains of the last wagon to survive on the estate were seen on a smoking bonfire next to the yard in 2006! Only the wheels and axles, together with the metal strapping and hinges from the wagon sides, survived. The wheel tread was measured as 2¼ inches and the flange depth as ¾ inch. The diameters of the wheels and the axles were 13 inches and 1½ inches respectively. The back-to-back distance between the flanges was 22 inches.

The main roles of the railway were to bring felled timber from the plantations to the sawmill, and to move the sawn timber, for example to the creosoting plant and the joiner's shop where gates and other items were made for sale to the public. In addition it was used to transport the foresters to and from their place of work at the start and end of every day. There were some small quarries of both limestone and whinstone on the estate and it is recorded that the line was occasionally used to remove some stone from these quarries, though details of the type of wagons used have not survived.

As well as serving on the Belford District Council and being a member of the Belford Board of Guardians, Colonel Leather took an active role in the Berwickshire Naturalists Club. His huge enthusiasm for trees and forestry resulted in his becoming a Member of the Royal English Arboricultural Society (REAS), which later became the Royal Forestry Society. He was its Vice-President by 1927 and was elected President in 1928.

He had created, at Middleton, 'a Mecca for those with forestry interests' and his estate and railway received numerous parties of visitors. One such visit took place on Tuesday 31st August, 1927 when members of the REAS made an inspection. After viewing the estate yard (where the sawmill with its moving table and 'pendulum crosscut saw' was in action) they watched some shunting as timber was being take in trucks to be stacked in the yard. Other wagons of timber were taken to the creosoting plant (powered by its gas engine making use of gas derived from sawdust). This plant had a tank measuring 24 ft x 6 ft and the timber was pressure-impregnated at 100 lb. per square inch. They inspected the small circular saw and band-saw which were electrically worked, the supply being generated by an 8 hp double vortex turbine with a 24 ft drop in water levels from the nearest of the lakes. The saws were being used to manufacture cart timbers ('felloes' and 'shafts') for which there was a good local demand. The joiners shop was also making gates, some of which were to be sold, the others being used on the estate. They also saw the suction gas plant and a 'Darfen' portable saw used for cutting firewood.

Half of the party then travelled by train, on wagons specially fitted with seats for the purpose, to inspect the Lake Cat Plantation whilst the train returned to the yard to collect the remainder. The full party next walked to inspect the 1914-planted rows of sitka spruce, pine and thuja. The train then transported the party to the far terminus at Detchant Wood where the larch, scots pine, douglas fir and Italian poplar trees were inspected at Naboth West and East Woods. Finally the party walked down the hillside, crossing the main road to the local station (Smeafield, LNER) to start their homeward journey.

Further similar visits took place until around 1938, the main form of transport being the railway, using the same flatbed wagons specially-adapted by the fitting of 'seats'. Post-World War II visits were made in estate cars, described in one account as 'rough riding'!

Further use was made of the railway's passenger carrying wagons on days when shooting parties visited the estate. For these events a train would first of all take the beaters up the line, then return for the 'guns'. A surviving photograph shows the line in use for a family outing or picnic. Alas, the locomotive broke down on this occasion. A proposed mineral railway on the Middleton Estate is described in a later book in this series.

Colonel Leather died in 1941 and his railway ceased to operate some time before the end of the war. In 1945 his son, Group Captain R.T. Leather, sold the Middleton Estate to the Greenwich Hospital (who owned other land in the north of Northumberland). The water-powered sawmill is known to have continued to operate until 1958 at least. The family forestry tradition was maintained on the Shielow Estate by his grandson, Colonel Mark Leather.

Colonel Leather's obituary, appearing in the *Royal Forestry Society Journal*, referred to his practical and professional management of the woods and the '...unforgettable impression left by the forest railway'.

Today we are fortunate as some early photographs of the line have been saved for posterity. Despite the recent (2007) sale of the estate the sawmill building is still in existence, and track and point work (with a point lever, made by Orenstein & Koppel) survive in the yard. Traces of rail survive elsewhere and the course of much of the trackbed can be followed with some ease, though most of it lies on private land and permission must be sought from the owners and lessees of the land before access can be gained. It is also advisable, additionally, to contact the local gamekeeper as gamebirds are reared, and shot, close to the route! Remains of several bridges and their abutments survive, though some vandalism has taken place associated with the recent cutting down of trees and land clearance in Swinhoe Strip, adjacent to Swinhoe Lane.

On the very day that the author visited the Middleton Hall yard the remains of the last timber wagon were still smouldering on a bonfire behind the sawmill building! Apart from the wheels and axles there were some items of metal strapping from the wagon sides and various parts of the brake system.   *Author*

Chapter Three

The Later Forestry and Timber Railways

As the story of Colonel Leather's railway, described in the last chapter, indicates, there was a continued demand for timber between the two World Wars. The woods around the village of Swarland, to the south of Alnwick, were extensive and contained many mature trees. This timber source was exploited in the mid-1930s and involved the use of a small railway.

In World War II several short-lived forestry or timber railways existed in the Rothley and Ewesley areas to the south and south-west of Rothbury. Two of these were situated between Gallows Hill and Rothley crossroads (now the B6342 road). The other was located close to Ewesley station on the LNER Rothbury branch. Another similar railway was located close to Chathill, north of Alnwick, whilst the Duke of Northumberland's Sawmill at Hulne Park, Alnwick, was served by a railway dating from the same period. Colonel Leather's railway at Middleton Hall, described in the last chapter, continued to work for much of the war.

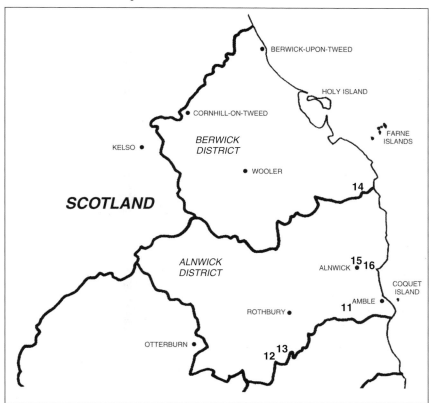

In this World War, as in the first, there was a need for much timber, both for military use and for use in the busy coalmines. Again, the traditional sources of timber, namely the states surrounding the Baltic Sea, were largely in the hands of the Axis powers and the Baltic ports were not available. As a result it was necessary to rely on home-grown timber. There was a further problem in that labour for cutting timber was sometimes in short supply as many men of suitable age were either enlisted into the forces or had 'reserved occupations' vital to other aspects of the war effort.

After the cessation of hostilities labour became more plentiful and extensive plantations of trees were established in the north of Northumberland, including Kielder Forest. The cutting down of mature trees continued and the Alnwick sawmill in Hulne Park, for example, continues to use timber from the Northumberland Estate for such tasks as the building of fences and gates. For some years a narrow gauge railway operated in the sawmill yard .

11 – The Swarland Wood Forestry Railway

Various local residents had suggested the existence of a forestry line in Swarland Woods, to the west of the A1 road, south of Alnwick. It was retired local forester Arthur Scott who was able to fill in the details for this short-lived railway.

The railway was constructed in the part of Swarland Wood known as 'Spring Wood' which largely contained hardwood trees, many being beech and oak. It operated some time between 1933 and 1935. The concern responsible for felling and sawing came from Sedgefield in County Durham, being called Thorburn (or Thoburn) & Kirkup. They operated three sawmills, two of which were served by rail lines. A firm of hauliers, believed to be called Ewarts of Morpeth, led the sawn timber from the wood using large lorries which were loaded by means of a sheerlegs crane. Some was transported as far south as Sheffield, whilst much was used in the shipbuilding industry of the North East, being cut into 3 in. to 6 in. chocks and wedges.

The total length of the railway was approximately one mile. One line led from the sawmill located towards the south end of Spring Wood, above the Swarland Burn (NU153027), up the hillside to the lorry loading point (NU161032) near the end of the 'Back Drive' leading to the South Lodge of the nearby Hall. The other track, a branch from the first, descended slightly from a second sawmill (NU155034) to a junction with the first line at the easterly corner of Spring Wood (NU 156029). A third sawmill, in the Hall grounds, was not rail-connected. These routes largely survive today though any remains of the lines have long-since disappeared.

The track, reported as being of '... about three foot' gauge, was laid with lightweight rails. At least two types of wagon were in use on the lines. The first type was for carrying lengths of tree trunk, these wagons having two four-wheeled bogies. The second type consisted of four-wheeled wooden-sided open wagons. These were for carrying smaller materials.

Sawn trunks were hauled to the sawmills either by horses or by means of steel cables hauled by winches and powered by stationary steam engines. The engines employed some of the felled timber, especially the smaller branches, as fuel. The rail wagons were hauled to the saw mills by horses, usually operating in pairs; no locomotives were involved. After completion of the contract the rails were lifted for use elsewhere.

Arthur Scott recalls evidence suggesting that there had been an earlier railway in, or near, the wood. He remembered that when he was a youngster there were some derelict axles and wheels, also the frames of 'an old bogie', lying in the wood. He was uncertain of their origin but these 'relics' may have been associated with the CWS Longframlington to Whittle Colliery cableway described earlier, being found not far from its former alignment.

Other local residents have suggested that another possible railway was located nearby, this being an early 19th century line associated with small quarries and a short-lived brickworks located near to Overgrass Farm, Swarland (NU150038). Clay from the 'pit' was taken to the brickworks and the bricks were subsequently transported along a line for the building of walls in the garden of Swarland Old Hall. Some earthworks may be the remains of this line.

However, none of these small lines can be identified on old OS maps and no photographs or documentary evidence has been discovered.

12 – The Rothley Forestry Railways

The first of the Rothley forestry lines was that which ran from the roadside near to Gallows Hill (NZ023895), to Greenleighton Wood and to the plantation named after the nearby Harwood House (NZ020920). The line was operated between 1943 and 1944. Laid with lightweight 2 ft gauge track, it was operated by a local man, Bill Wright, under contract to H.D. Ward of Wolsingham. The four-wheeled flat wagons employed to move the cut timber were hauled along the line by a Fordson tractor, the wheels of which straddled the narrow gauge track. Some horses were used in the woods where the timber was cut.

Several vehicles were used to bring the felled and cut timber to the line for loading and to remove timber from the roadside depot: these included a D4 Caterpillar, an International D9 diesel tractor and a small 2B Caterpillar. Local residents, including Albert Banks, 'Tucker' Priestly, Bill and Charlie Wright, Carl Crosier and I.T. Mackenzie (not called up for army service) worked here. Caravans at Greenleighton Wood provided their accommodation. Approximately six acres of woodland were felled for timber.

The present farmer at Greenleighton has reported that there are a few sleepers from the line still *in situ* in the wood and some rails, probably from this line, survive as fence posts. It is likely that the track from the roadside on the 1950s OS maps, running parallel to a boundary fence, is the alignment of part of this railway. Aerial photographs do not suggest an alternative route, though such a lightly-laid, unballasted and short-lived line is unlikely to have left much in the way of remains.

The second Rothley timber line was located a short distance to the east of the first one described above. It also commenced at the side of the road from Gallows Hill to Rothley crossroads (at NZ025896) but ran alongside the west edge of the Gallows Hill plantation to the timber-cutting site (NZ025903) on the east side of the Harwood Burn. This line was operated by the Ministry of

Supply between 1943 and 1944. The line was of 2 ft gauge and a small 4-wheeled diesel locomotive was reported to have hauled the timber wagons. This was referred to locally as the 'Tanky'. It has not been possible to identify this machine. The men employed here were housed in caravans, about five in number, located on a flat area close to the roadside. A local man, Joe Wake, is known to have provided a horse (called 'Britain') to pull felled timber to the line for loading onto wagons. This line has also left no obvious remains.

The land over which these two lines passed, and the plantations, are now in private ownership. However, a public bridleway follows the approximate line of the first railway from the B6342 road towards Greenleighton Farm. A branch from this bridleway heads towards Dyke Head Farm and passes within a few hundred yards of the Gallows Hill plantation.

13 – The Ewesley Forestry Railway

This line operated towards the end of World War II, though the precise dates of opening and closure have not been discovered. It has not been possible to find documents relating to the line and this account, as with the accounts of the two previously described lines, is based on the recollections of local residents.

Ewesley station (NZ059926) was located at the side of the Rothbury to Scots Gap road and was sited within the boundaries of an ancient earthwork. A bridge took the Rothbury branch railway over the road at this point, the abutments of which survive. At the time of the war the station had two sidings, one (about 350 yards in length) starting at the road bridge and being located opposite the station platform. The other, about 100 yards long, served a loading bank behind the platform. The first siding was used for passing trains when required; it was not a loop and a train had to 'set back' into the siding for passing purposes. Block post status was withdrawn in 1945 and this siding was removed by about 1950.

The station yard at Ewesley, on the former NBR's branch from Scots Gap to Rothbury, was the terminus of the short-lived, lightly-laid, World War II line which brought timber from 'Lake Wood' located to the south-east of the station.   *'Photos from the Fifties'*

The timber railway commenced in the station yard and ran 'down the Dene' on the land of farmer Jack Aynsley. The line headed east and then curved towards the south-east, finally south, along the edge of Lake Wood towards Ewesley Gill. It was the southern part of Lake Wood which was cut down (NZ069915). The line and timber-cutting operations were in the hands of Italian prisoners-of-war who were 'bussed in' from their nearby camp. It is believed that the timber wagons were horse-drawn on narrow gauge track. It is not known whether all of the timber was subsequently transferred to standard gauge rail wagons or whether some was transported away by road vehicles.

There are no on-the-ground remains of this lightly-laid and short-lived line, any small bridges over the burns having long-since disappeared. The site of the timber cutting, identifiable from the study of OS maps, has now been replanted and forms part of the Ewesley Plantation on the side of Broomfield Fell.

14 – The Chathill Forestry Railway

Chathill station, currently served by just four trains each weekday, lies on the East Coast Main Line between Alnmouth and Belford. It was formerly the junction for the North Sunderland Railway, the impecunious independent concern, which struggled, for many years, to provide a rail link between the main line and the settlements at North Sunderland and Seahouses. The story of this line has been told by Alan Wright in *The North Sunderland Railway* (Oakwood Press). However, the village of Chathill had another, albeit short-lived, railway during World War II.

It was in the very early 1940s that attention was turned to several plantations of mature coniferous trees that were located to the north-east of Chathill, adjacent to the road leading from the village and its station towards Swinhoe, and then onwards to the coast at Beadnell. To the north side of this road was located the Elymoor Plantation (NU190275), and to the south were found the Cottagefield and Tileshed Plantations (NU190272). The last of these was named after the former Chathill Tile Works, on whose former site the trees had been planted around the year 1900. (It has been suggested that this tile works had had its own railway or tramway for moving clay and for transporting wood for firing the kilns. However, no documentary evidence appears to exist and map evidence is inconclusive.)

An Australian forces unit was based at Annstead Camp near to Annstead Farm between Seahouses and Beadnell. Some of the men appear to have been billeted at Seahouses or at Beadnell, perhaps before the camp was ready to house them. It has not been, so far, possible to identify this unit with certainty, though official records show that several units of the specialist Australian Forestry Corps worked in England in the middle years of the war. According to information gleaned locally, the unit was primarily present for local defence purposes, for there was still a limited threat of invasion from the east, but was also employed in timber cutting, the workforce being moved between the camp and plantations by military road transport.

A temporary 2 ft gauge railway was laid in the plantations and several small four-wheeled wagons were used to move the cut logs to the nearby Chathill to Swinhoe road where a sawmill was located. Despite the relatively short distance involved, the narrow gauge line was not extended to Chathill station. Instead all of the cut timber was removed from the site by means of road vehicles and taken the 600 yards to Chathill station where it was transferred to rail wagons for onward movement on the main line. A small 4-wheeled Motor Rail 'Simplex' diesel locomotive, with mechanical transmission, number MR8735 (built in 1941) was delivered to the 'Timber Production Department, c/o Chathill Station', and it is believed that this locomotive provided the sole motive power for the railway. Several local residents can remember a small four-wheeled diesel locomotive hauling timber wagons at the site. One can recall the line passing 'tilesheds', the surviving buildings from the Chathill Tile Works. Unfortunately, no maps or plans appear to exist showing the extent of the rail system, though post-war OS maps indicate various footpaths or tracks, leading to the main road, along which the rails might have been laid. As with many such 'temporary' lines the rails would have been moved as the sites of tree cutting progressed through the various parts of the plantations. It is not known when work finished at the site but the plantations were completely stripped of their mature trees. The small locomotive was returned to the Motorail factory by 26th January, 1948, being sold on to Norwich Corporation. It was working at a sewage works at Kirby Bedon, near Norwich, by the middle of June 1948.

One interesting aspect of the tree-felling at this site is that the Australians, cutting the trees with axes, severed the trunks at shoulder height, some five feet above the ground, that is, they stood up whilst cutting, as was traditional in Australia (and in Canada). British woodcutting normally involved the men kneeling and cutting off the trunk close to ground level, thus obtaining more wood from each tree. At Chathill a group from the Women's Land Army (Forestry Section) was employed to 'clean up' the woods, firstly by reducing the trunks to ground level and secondly by removing the side branches which had been left behind by the Australians. It is not known if the railway was still operational to help them with this work.

Various local residents can remember some rails still being *in situ* until well after the end of the war behind the dwelling known as Swinhoe Cottage. Until the late 1980s some rails from the line survived in the hedge behind this building. These had been lifted from the ground and dumped when the adjacent field was deep-ploughed following the purchase of the land by the Northumberland Estates. Some cut-down sleepers, now in poor condition, which were incorporated into local fences, may have been from the line.

No on-the-ground remains of the line appear to survive today. However, study of aerial photographs of the area reveals 'marks' which might indicate the alignment of the railway close to the hedge behind, and at the side of, Swinhoe Cottage. Other similar markings cross the adjacent field. Both Elymoor and Tileshed Plantations have been replanted, though the former has not reached its pre-World War II size. This replanting has eliminated the possibility of remains of the line being revealed on present-day aerial photographs.

No photographs of the railway in operation have been discovered though some photographs displayed on an Australian Government website and showing a Simplex locomotive working at a forestry site 'somewhere in the North of England' give an impression of what it would have been like.

All of the land referred to is private and permission must be sought to visit it.

15 – The Alnwick Sawmill Railway

A short length of the railway at Alnwick Sawmill has survived into the 21st century. The mill is located to the west of Alnwick in Hulne Park adjacent to Park Cottage (NU 176139). It was constructed just after the start of the 20th century, its creosote plant, for preserving timber, being new in 1907. It originally produced pit props, reportedly mainly for the Hartlepool district. It is first shown on the OS maps of the 1920s. It is also known as 'Earl Percy's Sawmill' or the 'Estate Sawmill' (for it serves the Estate of the Duke of Northumberland).

The railway at the sawmill is believed to have been constructed around the time of the end of World War II, perhaps in 1945 or 1946. Its maximum length was about 100 yards. Originally it ran from a yard, where timber was stacked for drying, to a chipping plant with a siding leading to the creosote (pressure treatment) plant. Although rarely used latterly, the track remained *in situ* until the mid-1980s when most of it was concreted over. The only part visible today is the short section leading to the creosote, later Tanalising, plant where the softwood was treated to give it protection from fungal rot and insect attack. Initially there were two four-wheeled flat wagons on the line for taking timber to the creosoting plant. These were short, being of little more than two to three feet in length, with wheels of about 10 in. in diameter. In recent memory only one wagon was in use. Usually manpower was used to propel the wagons around the yard; in later years a tractor was occasionally used. The surviving rails are of 24½ in. gauge (measured to their inside edges, the distance between the rail centres being 26 in.

Today the short length of line is not used and its wagons have disappeared. The main work of the sawmill is to produce timber for fencing, much of it being used locally.

The public are allowed to walk along the tracks and paths in Hulne Park though permission must be sought at the office to approach the sawmill premises and inspect the remains of the line.

This 2009 photograph shows the full extent of the surviving part of this railway located at the estate sawmill in Hulne Park on the Duke of Northumberland's Estate. Formerly the rails led, via various items of pointwork, to a timber stack yard. Motive power was either manpower or tractor; no rail wagons have survived. *Author*

The narrow gauge lightweight rails of the Hulne Park sawmill railway are evident here. The short length of line, with its rails embedded in concrete, leads to a pressurized timber-treatment plant located behind the wooden gates. *Author*

16 – The Sanctuary Wood Sawmill Railway, Denwick, near Alnwick

In the early 1970s some trees were being cut down and timber removed from 'Sanctuary Wood', Denwick, to the east of Alnwick. To assist this, a short length of 2 ft gauge railway was laid to lead logs towards the small saw bench. Manpower was used to move the trucks. The line was no more than 100 yards in length and was in use for only about six months. It is believed that the sawmill was moved to a number of other locations locally and that some of the rail line may also have been moved to these locations. It is not known who operated the railway though it may have been workers from the Northumberland Estates.

Chapter Four

The Military Target Railways

Target railways have existed at three locations in the north of Northumberland. The first location was at Ross Links on the North Sea coast during World War II. This railway was relocated, in the 1950s, to a new site north of Redesdale Camp on the Army Ranges at Otterburn. Another target railway, using novel construction methods, was built later at a remote location known as 'White Spot', also at Otterburn.

17 – The Ross Links Target Railway

Ross Links is a remote, sparsely-populated area on the Northumberland coast in the Civil Parish of Middleton. It lies between the hamlet of Ross, and Ross Back Sands. From these sands views to the north encompass Holy Island, whilst to the south Bamburgh Castle can be seen beyond Budle Bay. The first military activity here was in 1899 when an Admiralty rifle range was operational. This was used by the 2nd Northumberland Volunteer Artillery and other units in World War I. Later, until 1925, there was an Admiralty wireless station at the site.

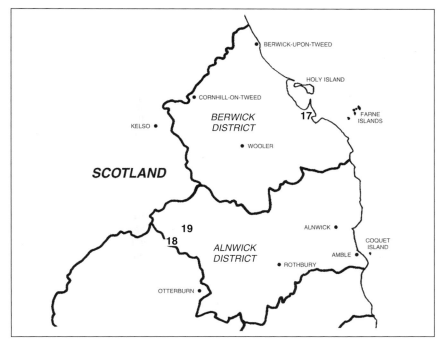

65

Plans for a target railway at Ross Links were drawn up in 1940 though the line was not constructed and operational until 1942. Being a time of war, there could be no opposition from 'the locals'. The purpose of the line was to provide moving targets for the firing of anti-tank rounds. Army units known to have trained here include:

Northern Units
631 anti-tank Regiment based at Scarborough
382 Regiment based at Halifax

Scottish Units
20 Regiment based at Gailes Camp, Troon, Ayrshire
254 Regiment based at Dumbarton
402 Regiment based at Greenock

The self-propelled target trolleys were stabled in a brick- and concrete-built trolley depot, which still exists (in agricultural use) in the early 21st century (NU137372). The depot, in which spare canvas targets were kept, had a single line of 2 ft 6 in. railway. As many as 11 different target trolleys may have operated at Ross Links at various times. All were 4-wheeled and built by Wickhams of Ware in Hertfordshire. They were powered by air cooled JAP petrol engines of 1,278 cc. Each of the trolleys had a wooden framework which allowed the attachment of the targets, made of canvas on a wooden frame. The targets had a black silhouette of a military tank and were readily replaced on the trolleys after successful firing. The works numbers of those known to have worked at Ross are: Wkm 3174/5/6/7, 3004, 3244/45 and 3285. It is probable that other Wickham trolleys were used at Ross Links, including Nos. 3172, 3246 and 3247.

The Wickham works lists show some trolleys, including 3245 and 3246, as being originally consigned to 'Buckton, Yorkshire (ER)'. However, there is no known target railway at this location or at Buckden, Yorkshire. However, Buckton in Northumberland is a hamlet very close to Smeafield, the nearest East Coast main line railway station to Ross Links.

The track layout at Ross was quite complex. After leaving the trolley depot or shed in a northerly direction the single line forked, with each fork leading onto the south balloon loop. From the north of the loop a single line extended northwards towards the most northerly of the balloon loops (which permitted trolleys to change direction without stopping if necessary). Two other lines led from this loop: a line heading in a south-easterly direction towards the third balloon loop and a final line leading south-south-east to the fourth balloon loop. Close to the most northerly loop were several points and connections allowing trolleys to be exchanged between the various parts of the system. Altogether there were several thousand yards of track. This was constructed from lightweight rails spiked directly to wooden sleepers. 'Trips' between the rails engaged with levers on the trolleys to regulate their movement.

The whole system, referred to on contemporary OS maps as a 'Mineral Railway' (no doubt for security reasons!) was located on a stretch of the links known as Long Bog, mostly less than 20 ft above ordnance datum. The entire army range covered some 1,136 acres with its 'danger area' extending out to sea for 12,000 yards on a huge arc between Holy Island and the Farne Islands. Near to the railway were several observation towers, bunkers, pill boxes and other military buildings. Firing towards the moving targets was always in the direction of the sea to prevent stray rounds from harming persons, grazing animals or property inland. The dunes were meant to act as a 'backstop' to prevent stray rounds from travelling out to sea! However, shipping was banned from the immediate area beyond the dunes and beach.

The system operated successfully through the last years of World War II. However, once hostilities had finished the army wished to continue firing at the site. After the closure of similar ranges at Kimmeridge on the Isle of Purbeck and at Harlech, the army claimed that the two surviving ranges at Ross Links and at Lydd were still vital for their training needs. Alternative locations, including Redesdale, Larkhill, Okehampton, Sennybridge, Warcop, Bovington, Castle Martin and Kirkcudbright were dismissed on the grounds that they were already fully used. Local objections to the continuation of firing were wide-ranging and vociferous; the reasons for objection included the following:

- interference with agriculture and the frightening of livestock
- religious grounds (the Holy Island of Lindisfarne was nearby)
- fishing and shipping (fisherman from several local ports used the fishing grounds off this part of the coast)
- the effect on wildlife including birds, the effect on tourism
- the need for the protection of amenities (for sailing and walking)

Objectors included the Lord Bishop of Newcastle and the Archbishop of York, local farmers and fishermen, local dignitaries, and organized groups (such as trade unions, the RNLI, Trinity House, the Ramblers Association, local Naturalist groups and Women's Institute branches). The matter was referred to the Prime Minister, Clement Attlee, who raised the issue in Cabinet. The Cabinet commissioned a full public enquiry which was held in Newcastle under the auspices of Sir Geoffrey Whiskard on 16th June, 1948. The army case was proposed by the Chief of Staff, Northern Command, (chosen, it is said, specifically to impress the Lord Bishop as Sir Geoffrey was a very religious man!). The decision of the Public Enquiry, passed to the Cabinet, was unanimous, with Herbert Morrison then, somewhat mischievously, informing the Archbishop of Canterbury (not York!) that approval of the continuation of firing would be granted for Mondays to Fridays only, so as not to interfere with religious activities on Holy Island. Most of the firing would take place in summer. A strict limit of four guns firing at one time would be enforced. All of the other objections were not considered to be relevant or valid.

The target railway system thus continued its operations until 1956-58 when space became available towards the north end of Redesdale Camp and the Ross system was lifted and removed there. The absence of new detailed surveys of Ross Links meant that the system still appeared there on OS maps until the late 1970s. Aerial photographs taken at the start of the 21st century permit the identification of most of the former layout. Two remaining features prominent on current maps are the trolley depot, now used for storage by the local farmer, and the route of the south-east line and loop which have become used as a land drain, a small pond having formed to the west of the loop. Much of the system now lies on private land to which there is no public access without permission from the landowner. In any case cars must be parked at the entrance to Ross village (in the roadside car park just before 'The West House'). A 10 minute walk passing through the village and along a gated track as far as the former Coastguard Cottages allows access to Ross Links. The former trolley depot with its curved roof can be seen to the right and the earthworks of the first loop can be discerned especially in dry conditions. The high dunes further on allow surveillance of much of the rest of the site of the target railway system. The whole area has now been designated as a Special Area of Conservation (SAC) and is regularly patrolled and monitored by wardens.

Several recently-published references have been made to a possible fighter-bomber aircraft training range located to the north of Ross Links at Goswick Sands, operational in the last year of World War II. This is reputed to have had a 10 ft square moving target for aircraft with 20 mm cannons, also a section of railway line 'for rocket projectile attacks'. It is not known if the targets were moved by trolley or by winch haulage. Whilst the military had certainly occupied Goswick Sands since the end of the 19th century (when there was a rifle range, officers mess and other buildings at the site) the OS maps show no evidence or detail of such a line and it has not been possible to obtain further information of this possibly short-lived railway. Military authorities and the National Archive appear to have no records of a railway here.

This photograph, taken in 2009, shows the surviving 'depot' or trolley shed at Ross Links. It is now in agricultural use for the housing of livestock and their feed. Traces of the former trackbed on land with public access are traceable especially after a period of dry weather conditions.   *Author*

18 – The Silloans Target Railway near Redesdale Camp

The Ministry of Defence ranges at Otterburn and Redesdale are located between Upper Coquetdale and the A68 trunk road. They have provided, since before World War I, sites for infantry training. Later, as military technology advanced, they have been used for training for tank warfare and have been the location of artillery ranges (including those for the firing of anti-tank rounds, and, more recently, rockets). A demolition range also exists at Bellshiel. The old Roman road known as Dere Street crosses the ranges; it is now metalled and forms a route for both military and agricultural vehicles. Other archaeological remains include ancient burial mounds and the remains of World War I practice trenches! Strictly speaking, the target railway at Silloans lies a few hundred yards outside the boundary of the Alnwick District. However, the fact that it was formerly located within the north of Northumberland merits its inclusion here.

It was in 1956 that some of the target trolleys and track were moved from Ross Links to a new site (NT827016), between Dere Street and Silloans Farm just to the east of the old Roman road, and adjacent to the army road leading to Bushman's Crag. Some items were placed in store for a short period as the construction of the new line was not completed until 1961. The railway is officially known as the 'Silloans Moving Target System'.

The system constructed was greatly simplified compared to that at Ross Links. Initially it used some of the lightweight track that had been lifted from Ross. The gauge remained at 2 ft 6 in. and the track was spiked to the wooden sleepers (though later some heavier weight track with concrete sleepers was used). It is not known for certain how many of the Wickham trolleys were moved from Ross to Silloans. A private individual purchased Wkm 3174 and 3175 from here when they were made redundant, being then renumbered L4135 and L4134 respectively. Others from the original JAP-engined series are believed to have been 3245 and one from Wkm 3004, 3176, 3244 and 3285. A visit in 1986 revealed three of the original trolleys, two in full working order with the other partly cannibalized for spares. In 2003 a further visit revealed five trolleys on site, though only one of these, Wkm 3245/1943, was an original. This retained its original JAP engine but was not in operational condition, being badly rusted. Four newer trolleys were present in 2003. These were Wkm 11686-9, all built in 1990 and fitted with Volkswagen petrol engines. All the trolleys have a drive onto just one of the trolley axles and their wheel arrangement, in railway parlance, is thus 2w-2PM. Today all of the new trolleys carry a single digit 'running number' on their control panels corresponding to the last digit of their works number; the working trolleys are thus numbered 6, 7, 8 and 9.

As originally laid in the 1950s on the site of a former tank range, the rail system took the form of a dumb-bell shape with a central double-track section and balloon loops at each end. The trolleys would thus pass the firing zone twice in one circuit of the track. Later the layout was modified to have just a single-track central system but retaining the balloon loops. At some early stage the position of the balloon loops was modified, perhaps to reduce the sharpness of the curvature. In the 1990s the layout was radically changed. The balloon loops were lifted and the system was converted into a squashed oval shape with continuous running (in an anti-clockwise direction). The length of the circuit is

This photograph was taken inside the trolley depot at Silloans during a society visit. It shows several target trolleys, including, in the foreground, the one surviving Wickham trolley dating from World War II which has a JAP engine. The other, more modern trolleys, are powered by Volkswagen engines.   *Author*

On the occasion of an 'official' railway society visit a Wickham target trolley is posed, complete with both anti-tank and infantry targets, outside the trolley shed. The shed is located towards the end of the only siding on the Silloans railway system.   *Author*

Right: A target trolley propels itself around the Silloans railway system. On the downhill parts the trolley 'freewheels' whilst for the uphill sections trips between the rails cause the clutch to become re-engaged. A manual lever allows the vehicles to be halted as they pass the shed siding.
Author

Below: Apart from the target trolleys there is just one item of rolling stock at Silloans, namely this Hudson-built wagon with low sides, currently out-of-use. The 'main line' can be seen behind the wagon; one of the 'control trips' can be seen between the rails above the left-hand end of the wagon.
Author

now said to be about 600 metres. A siding constructed close to the main road leads to a depot (NT 827016) with a door at each end, a single track and semi-circular roof outline. A control bunker is located nearby. The trolleys are stored in the depot away from the inclement weather, and spare targets, both for the railway and infantry training, are stacked against the walls. At the far end of the depot a track leads outside to a small turntable. Short spurs from this allow the trolleys to be transferred to and from road vehicles if necessary. The only item of rolling stock apart from the trolleys is an old, small, flat bed wagon, built by Hudson's, which was, until recently, found on some rough ground adjacent to the depot. Its former purpose is unknown.

Control of the trolleys is by means of trips set between the rails which make contact with a lever on the trolley underframe as it passes. This connects or disconnects the drive from the gearbox to the wheels allowing the vehicles to been driven under power or to coast (especially on the downhill sections). The vehicles are unmanned when operating. As formerly at Ross Links, they bear wooden frames to which large canvas targets, in the form of an outline of a black tank, can be attached. The line runs in a shallow cutting throughout most of its length so that the inert rounds fired do not damage the trolleys themselves. Only one trolley is used at any time.

In the mid-1980s it was forecast that the line had little future as a result of changes in weaponry. However, it was considered wise to purchase new trolleys as a result of the age and deteriorating condition of the originals. At the start of the 21st century, despite the closure of the administrative buildings at Redesdale and supervision being transferred to Otterburn Camp, the railway was still in use on several occasions each year and all four of the 'modern' trolleys were in good working order. In 2006 and 2007 visits to the line at 'non-firing' times have occasionally revealed a shiny top to the roadside rails, indicating recent use. However, by early 2010 the line appeared not to have been used for some time, with mud and animal droppings partly covering the track leading from the depot. The operation of the line is supervised by the Range Wardens now based at Otterburn Camp.

It must be emphasised that this railway is located on Ministry of Defence land and no access is possible in the 'prohibited periods' when the display of red flags indicates that firing is in progress.

Numerous signs warn against the dangers of trespass, especially if straying from the roads. If the red flags are *not* displayed then the public have access to much of the range complex in their vehicles and it is possible to see part of the target railway from the roadside. The dates and times when the ranges are 'open' are publicized in the local press and on various noticeboards in the area. If in doubt it is best to contact the Ministry of Defence Liaison & Access Officer for the camp.

19 – The White Spot Target Railway

During an organized visit to the Silloans system in 2003, it was mentioned by one of the MoD staff that another target railway, described at the time as a 'monorail', was located deep within the central area of the Otterburn Range, but that, in view of its position and the risks involved, it would not be possible for a visit to be made to this site. However, a couple of years later a visit was made by a very small party under strict instructions and supervision. The area was specially 'swept' of live ordnance before the visit.

It must be emphasised that this site is located in a Danger Area designated for live firing and under no circumstances should any attempt be made by private individuals or groups to visit it by vehicle or on foot. Signs clearly indicate that access by the public is prohibited. Red flags are displayed when firing is in progress and access to this part of the ranges is wholly prohibited.

In the early 1980s the UK land forces required a moving target system to be incorporated into the Otterburn Training Area infrastructure. It is known as the 'Milan System'.

The line runs from a small depot at White Spot (NT862046) to a military parking place at Black Knowe, north of Bluestone Edge (NT857043) close to a tributary of the Wilkwood Burn. It lies about 300 metres above sea level. It is around 500 metres in length and consists of two fairly straight lengths of track joined by a sharp bend. There is evidence close to this bend that the line was originally shorter with a straight track layout. The area beyond the curve, towards White Spot rocks appears to be of a slightly later construction. It was designed and manufactured by Saab in the early 1980s. Installation was carried out by British Army 'Sappers'. Track construction began on 15th April, 1986 and the first live round was fired on 14th May of the same year.

This photograph was taken at the upper end of the line inside the covered shed which accommodates the target trolley when it is not in use. The method of placing the expanded polystyrene targets on the trolley can be seen. Unfortunately the haulage vehicle was locked away during this arranged visit. *Author*

This photograph of the White Spot Target Railway was taken during an arranged visit. It shows the terminal straight section at the lower end of the line with the braking system for the trolley visible between the rails. The elevated nature of the line is evident as is the unusual rail section.
William Stafford

Also taken during an arranged visit to this line this dramatic shot shows a distant derelict army tank and the uneven nature of the Saab-designed elevated 'Milan System' railway on which the solitary target trolley runs.
William Stafford

It is certainly not a monorail, but has an equally unusual form of construction, being an elevated railway! It has this form so that, despite the deep snow often experienced in this part of Northumberland, it will normally be available for use. The rails take the form of square section steel-mounted with a diagonal axis vertical. They are supported about 70 cm above the ground on a series of trestles. The gauge, measured between the corners of the steel section, is 1 metre. The rolling stock for the line consists of a 4-wheeled petrol-engined trolley (not visible at the time of the visit as it was locked inside the large container which serves as a depot, store and workshop at White Spot), and target-carrying wagons with double-flanged wheels, housed, when not in use, beneath a rudimentary shelter. The powered trolley was said to be of about the same size as the Wickham trolleys at Silloans; it was reported, but not confirmed by inspection, that it has a Saab engine. The target-carrying wagons are 4-wheeled and just over three metres in length. They carry electrical heating elements. Once 'warmed up', large 8 ft x 4 ft white polystyrene sheets are attached to the outside of the wagon. The wagon is then released and it descends by gravity down the gradient. Meanwhile 'Apache' helicopters fire their heat-seeking missiles at the polystyrene targets. On reaching the end of the line the wagon is braked to a stand by means of trips between the rails. The powered trolley then descends, attaches a steel cable to the wagon and hauls it back up the gradient.

The worn rail 'corners' and the large numbers of polystyrene pieces (and spent missiles) lying in the vicinity indicated that the line had been recently used though the tops of the rails had quickly rusted in the recent wet weather.

The line was first indicated, in outline, on the 1980s-surveyed OS maps and is marked as a railway on low-scale modern maps. Strangely it is not marked as a railway on large scale maps of the area. In view of the likely future use of attack helicopters it is likely that the line will continue to be used.

This is a close-up view of the double-flanged wheels of the White Spot target trolley. At the time that the photograph was taken the wheels were rather rusty, suggesting that the railway had not been in use for a short time. However, in this very exposed location it does not take long for rust to form!   *Author*

Chapter Five

The Passenger-Carrying Railways
near Berwick

Two passenger-carrying 'pleasure railways' have operated in the Berwick District, whilst a third was planned but not built. The first of these was an extremely short-lived miniature railway which operated on the seafront at Spittal Promenade in 1966, whilst the second, the Heatherslaw Light Railway, continues to operate very successfully, between stations at Ford Forge, near Heatherslaw Mill, and Etal, the village which is famous for having the only thatched pub in Northumberland! The proposed line at Seahouses is dealt with in another chapter.

20 – The Spittal Miniature Railway

Spittal, south of Tweedmouth on the Northumberland coast, has a beach and promenade, and is popular with 'locals' and some visitors. In 1966 a local resident, John Harrison, of Osborne Road, Tweedmouth, purchased a locomotive, carriages and track for a miniature railway which he laid at the southern end of Spittal Promenade on some derelict land in front of Martins printing works. Additionally he planned to gain a small income from parking charges for vehicles on the land not occupied by the miniature railway. John, originally from Yorkshire, had, with his wife, formerly operated the refreshment room at Berwick railway station and had managed an ice-cream and sweet stall at Spittal Promenade.

The track for the railway was of 12 in. gauge. It was laid in an oval pattern, with a small shed being provided for the single locomotive, a 4-4-2 tender engine named *Prince Edward*. This locomotive had been built in 1935 by a Mr G. Flooks. It had two outside cylinders measuring 2½ in. by 4½ in. Its driving wheels were 13 inches in diameter and the tender had eight wheels. The locomotive was painted in a light olive green livery. It had formerly operated at the Ruislip Lido Railway in London until 1959 but its whereabouts, until it 'reappeared' at Spittal in 1966, are not confirmed. It was purchased by Harrison 'in working order' but on arrival in Northumberland it was taken to the engineering factory of J.H. ('Jimmy') Woods at West End, Tweedmouth, where it was refurbished. The tender remained at Spittal. The locomotive was steamed at Spittal on 'anthracite eggs', though these did not prove to be an ideal fuel. The engine ran trials though it is believed that it hardly ran carrying members of the paying public.

Two 'toast rack' bogie carriages were purchased at the same time as the locomotive. These had eight transverse benches seating two persons side-by-side. The backs of the seats could be 'swivelled' so that passengers could face in either direction. The carriages carried plates indicating that they were built by 'Clarkson, York, 1963'.

The year 1966 was definitely not a good one to have chosen to open a miniature railway at Spittal! The incessant rain at Easter produced local flooding. Then, in the late spring, three young children were drowned on the beach. This tragic event led the local council to advise that children should not bathe here, especially within a couple of hours each side of the time of high tide.

Taken near the Promenade at Spittal, near Berwick, in 1966, this photograph shows the Spittal Miniature Railway under construction. In the foreground is one of the line's two toast-rack carriages whilst beneath the tarpaulin is the tender for the line's 4-4-2 steam locomotive *Prince Edward* which was away at an engineering factory at Tweedmouth for repair and refurbishment.   *Beamish Museum Collection*

The local newspaper reported that various youth groups, including Sunday Schools, that had traditionally visited Spittal for their annual day out or picnic, had decided to make alternative arrangements, some, for example, visiting Coldstream instead. In addition, in mid-summer, a large storm deposited much seaweed and debris on Spittal beach. It was some time before the council could arrange to have this cleared, resulting in complaints of smells and flies. August then turned out to be the wettest for over 10 years! The *Berwick Advertiser* reported that the gentleman who held the licence for providing donkey rides on the beach had asked the council for a refund of part of his licence fee as the summer had been such a disastrous one and he had not made a profit.

It was against this background that Harrison had built his railway! He planned to operate it with the assistance of a former locomotive driver from Tweedmouth depot. In the event the line's existence was short-lived and it was taken up at the end of the 1966 summer season, though the event was not reported in the local newspaper. By 1967 he had moved the materials and stock down to a park in Ilkley in Yorkshire where the Olicana Miniature Railway was located. In the 1970s some houses were built on the railway's former site at Spittal. The locomotive was believed, in 2004, to be with a private owner in Mablethorpe, Lincolnshire. No photographs of it in action at Spittal have yet come to light. However, the photograph shows one of the carriages, and the locomotive tender largely concealed under a tarpaulin, at the time that the locomotive was away for repair.

21 – The Heatherslaw Light Railway

This light railway operates between two terminus stations at Ford Forge (NT933384) and Etal (NT925393). It lies in the middle of the estate of Lord Joicey. The line's operational base is at Ford Forge on the opposite side of the River Till from Heatherslaw Mill, a working water mill. The line is about 12 miles from Berwick-upon-Tweed and can be approached via the B6354 road. Visitors approaching from Coldstream (six miles distant) and Wooler (eight miles distant) can follow the route signposted from the A697 road. There are bus services from both Berwick and the Borders which pass close to the railway. The line is very attractive and well worth a visit.

The gauge of the line is 15 in. and it has 3.2 km of track, having been extended in 2005. It is laid with flat-bottomed rail spiked directly to wooden sleepers. The line starts at Ford Forge where the station has a single passenger platform with an awning and a small booking office which serves as a shop and sells some souvenirs as well as train tickets. There is plenty of car parking in the station yard and coach parking on the roadside outside the station site.

Trains leave the station and pass beneath a metal road bridge which carries traffic for Heatherslaw Mill and Crookham village. The track is laid on a ledge between fields and the river bank. Shortly the line emerges into pasture land. At this point the single line formerly curved to the right, heading in a northerly direction directly towards Etal. During the 2005 works the line was extended to continue to follow the river westwards, crossing West Haugh, a flat area of grazing land. A cattle grid is crossed before the line's passing loop is reached. This is located on the opposite side of the river from Crookham village. Here the line curves and, still following the river, it heads in an easterly direction. Plantations of young trees hide the river for some of this length. Parts of the ground in this vicinity are rather wet and the line has been raised up on shallow wooden 'viaducts'. Further on the route joins the old alignment, the foundations of which can be discerned crossing the meadow on the right-hand side. Here the line crosses another cattle grid, climbs through a small cutting and then crosses the points into Etal station, located on Castle Bank below the castle and the Old Manse. At Etal village, a short walk away, there is Northumberland's only thatched pub, the 'Black Bull', which serves drinks, lunches and other refreshments. There is also a café, a small plant nursery, a blacksmith's forge, a woodturning workshop and a delightful cricket ground, plus the imposing Etal Castle. Car parking is available near the castle for those who wish to join the train at this end of the line.

Etal station is provided with a single platform on the running line and there is a run-round loop used by the locomotive to access the other end of its train. At the village end of the platform is found the turntable for turning the train's engine and allowing access to the loop; on this railway the steam locomotive always makes its journeys smokebox leading. Already the original turntable has been replaced by a longer one which will be capable of accommodating the line's second steam locomotive which will be longer than *The Lady Augusta*. No other station facilities, apart from a few seats, are provided at the station, though a gated footpath leads to the nearby castle and village.

At the Ford Forge end of the line there is a similar turntable but this has several exit roads, giving access to some sidings and the loco shed, as well as the run-round loop. Other sidings, on the river side of the site, are accessed from the run-round loop. The sidings house a crane, service vehicles, spare carriages and, usually, the diesel engine, though this is often stabled beneath the station canopy. The steam locomotive's watering facility is provided at Ford Forge, as is its wood and coal fuel.

The usual train locomotive was until recently *The Lady Augusta*, an outside-cylindered 0-4-2 built by Brian Taylor. It arrived from Ravenglass in 1989. It burns solid fuel (including small logs) and its boiler has a working pressure of 185 lb. per square inch. Its cylinders measure 6 in. by 5 in. It is fitted with Walschaerts valve gear operating slide valves. It has manganese steel tyres on its wheels to improve wear. Perhaps its main claim to fame is that it was, when built, the only steam locomotive to be fitted with disc brakes! It can haul a maximum load of 20 tons up a maximum gradient of 1 in 35. It is fitted with a half cab, the driver being seated on the front part of the tender.

The second locomotive is named *Clive*. It was originally a six-wheeled petrol-hydraulic machine (the frames of which are now under the line's mobile crane) but parts (for example the engine, transmission and some body parts) were used to build a 'new' Bo-4 locomotive. Originally built by Neville Smith in 1989, it was 'rebuilt' at Heatherslaw and is the standby locomotive. It was also the second locomotive, formerly used when two trains were running during peak periods of traffic. In future its use will be as 'standby' locomotive or for use on works trains. (Prior to

The bright sunlight creates dark shadows beneath *The Lady Augusta* which rests in the station at Etal station prior to departure for Ford Forge at Heatherslaw. The single platform, close to the River Till and Etal Castle, is provided with seats but there is no shelter (except in the carriages) in the event of inclement weather.   *Author*

In late summer 2009 the 0-4-2 *The Lady Augusta* was still the Heatherslaw Railway's only steam locomotive. In its usual immaculate external condition it is shown at the platform end at Etal awaiting the return to Ford Forge with a lightly-loaded train. A couple of weeks after this picture was taken the line was to be devastated by floods.   *Author*

building the 15 in. gauge line at Heatherslaw, Mr Smith had built and operated trains on a private 7¼ in. gauge miniature railway at his smithy home, not far away.)

The part-completed third locomotive was recently finished by Alan Keef Ltd at Lea Link in the Forest of Dean. The locomotive, in blue livery, was delivered to Heatherslaw on 11th June, 2010. It has been named *Bunty* after a competition had been held between 1st July and 21st August, 2009 inviting the public to choose its name. This locomotive is designed to be environmentally friendly, burning a renewable resource: timber. Its boiler pressure is 200 lb. per square inch and it has superheaters fitted. A fully enclosed cab should make life easier for the drivers on wet days. Its official launch date was 2nd July, 2010, its first train being sent on its way by the Rt Hon. Alan Beith MP who was present at the launch of the line in 1989. At the same time two new coaches, built at the railway's own workshops, entered service.

There are currently almost 20 passenger carriages, each carrying up to 20 passengers, in service on the line; these permit excellent views over the river and the pastures. They are wide enough to permit two passengers to travel side by side. The line's publicity brochure refers to the swans, moorhens, herons and kingfishers which can be seen from the train, though to this can be added robins, pheasants, crows, mallard ducks and coots, not to mention the seasonal wild flowers. The fields on the Haugh regularly contain cattle or sheep. There is no doubt that this is a very scenic line. There is easy access for those in wheelchairs (though the car park is gravelled) and dogs are carried free.

A return journey on the line takes about 45 minutes inclusive of the stop at Etal. Services run hourly from 11 am to 3 pm from Ford Forge between March and October, and in July and August from 11 am to 4 pm. The return journeys from Etal start on the half hour. Supplementary trains may be run if there is a demand at 'peak periods' in the summer, provided the necessary staff are available! These trains start from Ford Forge on the half hour and return from Etal on the hour. The two trains pass in the passing loop on the Haugh. The points at this loop are sprung so that it is not necessary for train crews to change them.

At Easter the line operates 'Easter Specials' and on occasions there are 'Teddy Bear Treasure Hunts' and Halloween events for the children. Just before Christmas there are the annual 'Santa Specials'. These operate during two weekends, on both Saturdays and Sundays. Currently run by Mrs Bernice Smith and her son Paul, the line is justly popular and hosts between 25,000 and 30,000 visitors each year. For the enthusiast the railway offers train-driving courses.

At the Ford Forge end of the line there is the railway's shop located in the booking office. There are also two model railways, one each of 'OO' and 'G' gauges. The nearby Heatherslaw Mill is a listed building with two water wheels, one of which operates. It has a tea room and shop and tourist information and toilets are available. These facilities are approached via the metal road bridge which crosses over the railway. Not far away is the delightful Ford village with the Lady Waterford Hall and garden centre.

The proximity of the line to the River Till has posed some problems on several occasions. In 1992, for example, the water level rose to such an extent that part of the trackbed was covered. Fortunately the damage to the track was not too serious and a full train service was soon reintroduced.

A far more serious flood occurred at the beginning of September 2008 when the river reached, officially, 71 cm above its 1948 level, which was previously the highest recorded. In 2008, as recorded by local press photographers, the water reached to the roof level of the coaches parked in the station sidings! The locomotive *The Lady Augusta* was locked inside the locomotive shed and the water level reached almost half way up the smokebox. Fortunately, by a matter of only ¼ in. it failed to overflow into the blastpipe and thence, via the steam pipes, into the cylinders. Silt, suspended in the water, could have caused much damage. As it was, much work was required, initially using a high pressure water jet, to enable it to return to service. The locomotive *Clive*, parked in the yard, also suffered water damage. Before it was able to be put back in service it was necessary to drain and replace all of its oils, including that from the hydraulic transmission. Remarkably its sealed batteries suffered no damage. Many hours of work were performed on this locomotive, too.

The trackbed also suffered much damage. In the 'Cut', where the alignment runs on a ledge above the river close to Heatherslaw, much sand and vegetation was deposited but his required only a fraction of the work needed on the Haugh where the Till's raging current had destroyed the river banks leaving a section of the track suspended in mid-air. Material was dumped to fill the gap in part, but it was necessary, over a length of over 40 metres, to move the alignment of the trackbed away from the river and relay ballast and track. Other remedial work, involving replacement of heavy timbers, was necessary on the Etal side of the line's passing loop where the line is carried on a low 'viaduct' above some marshy and uneven ground. It was also necessary for substantial trackwork on the bank below Etal station where the ballast had been washed away and the track damaged.

Clive, pictured here at Heatherslaw in the summer of 2010, was formerly used on 'extra' trains at the height of the summer holiday season and also provided the motive power for engineering trains. With the arrival of *Bunty* it will in future rarely appear at the head of passenger trains.   *Author*

The Heatherslaw Light Railway's second steam locomotive *Bunty* makes its departure from the Etal terminus with a good complement of passengers in August 2010. *The Lady Augusta*, the line's first steam locomotive, was rostered for the haulage of the 'extra' passenger trains at the height of the summer season (mainly mid-week days in August).

Author

At the start of October work had progressed to such an extent that a limited train service could be started. This consisted of a push-pull train, operated by the diesel locomotive, which operated over the first third of the line from the Heatherslaw, Ford Forge, end. Remarkably a full service was reintroduced for the school 'half term week' towards the end of the same month. A six-coach train was being hauled by *The Lady Augusta* albeit with some severe speed restrictions where the trackbed needed further consolidation. Much debris remained at the trackside, on the fences, in the fields and on the riverbank.

Much chaos was also caused at the site of the Heatherslaw Mill, shop and tea room. These, like the railway, had reopened by the time of the return of the train service, though for a time they were able to offer only limited facilities, the tea shop, for example, being able only to offer light refreshments rather than the usual meal service.

The floods were to return in 2009! On 17th July the Environment Agency issued a flood alert for the River Till. The river level rose and water spilled onto parts of the railway's track, washing away some sections of ballast. Though it was necessary to cease operations for three days, hard work by the staff enabled a part-service to be resumed by the 21st July with a full service being operated on the 22nd. The floods, fortunately, did not prove to be as serious as those of the previous September. Paul Smith expressed his relief, saying that the line could not have afforded to lose the revenue from the July traffic.

On 1st July, 2009 the line celebrated its 20th year of operation. Additional '20th year' celebrations were arranged for 29th to 31st August, including an exhibition at Heatherslaw depicting the 20 years of operation of the line. This formed part of the 'Stephenson 150 Festival' organized by Berwick Museum and supported by other groups. The series of events was arranged to commemorate the 150th Anniversary of the death of the celebrated engineer, Robert Stephenson. Simultaneously, and near to the Heatherslaw line, the Etal Village Hall housed an exhibition of local railway history.

Chapter Six

Contractors' Railways

In his book *The Railway Navvies*, author Terry Coleman wrote:

It takes many men - with ideas, and engineering know-how, and shovels to build a railway, and the method of executing works by contract and sub-contract was essential to the sudden and rapid growth of the nineteenth century.

To the word 'railway' he could have added other large engineering works such as piers, docks and harbours, reservoirs and estates of industrial housing.

Whilst the northern part of Northumberland was, and still is, largely rural, its pastoral landscape was to become crossed by various major railways and roads linking England to Scotland. Its sparse population meant that opposition to the building of water reservoirs for the large conurbations to the south was minimal so that several, of large size, were constructed in the region. Finally the minerals and other natural resources demanded outlets and hence ports and harbours were constructed and enlarged. It was the various contracting firms, with their access to specialist equipment and teams of mobile labour that often executed such works, regularly using small railways to facilitate their work.

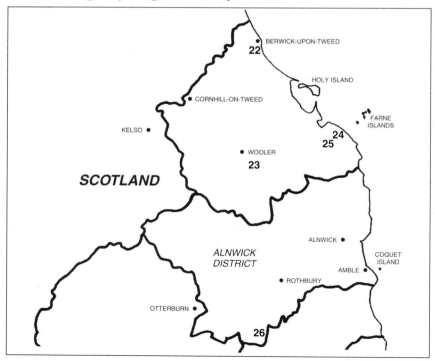

22 – McKay & Blackstock's Royal Border Bridge Contractor's Railways

The contract for the building of the Royal Border Bridge (NT993533), designed by Robert Stephenson to carry the Newcastle & Berwick Railway over the River Tweed from Tweedmouth, on the south bank, to Berwick, on the north bank, was let in November 1846. The appointed contractor was James McKay & J. Blackstock (of Cumberland) and its Resident Engineer was George (later Sir George) Barclay Bruce, assisted by Thomas Elliott Harrison. James Carstairs was in charge of the purchase of materials and the paying of the labour force. In 1851 Bruce presented a paper to the Institute of Civil Engineers, entitled *Description of the Royal Border Bridge over the River Tweed on the York, Newcastle and Berwick Railway,* and this provides valuable insight into aspects of its construction.

So as to advance the date of the entry of trains into Berwick station from the south a temporary wooden trestle bridge was constructed to the east of the planned alignment of the stone bridge (actually a viaduct). This structure was 1,666 ft-long and had a height of 125 ft. The trestle bridge required 76,627 cubic feet of timber for its construction and was built at a cost of £14,340. It came into use on 10th October, 1848. A drawing of this bridge, showing a locomotive-hauled train passing over it, is kept in Berwick Museum. It was drawn in July 1850, just one month before the completion of the adjacent stone structure; work on the last arch had been put into place on 26th March of that year but work continued on the decking and trackbed until August.

The foundation stone for the viaduct had been laid on 15th May, 1847. By then the contractor had already set up a yard in Tweedmouth on the south side of the river. This yard received rough blocks of stone from the local quarries. A team of masons dressed the stone here. In addition lime from the limeworks at both Lowick and Scremerston was also brought to this yard, as were sand and the rubble used as infill within the stone piers of the viaduct. Rails were laid by the contractor for moving materials from the yard, first of all temporary lines for the construction of the viaduct's approach embankment and then for the viaduct itself. Some 760,000 cubic yards of material were tipped to form the embankment and six small tramway lines were planned to convey the wagonloads of material to the tipping points. In the event just four lines were actually used. In one 'record' week some 5,765 wagonloads of materials were tipped to extend the embankment.

Many of the stone piers for the bridge, or viaduct, were laid upon 'floors' which were laid within coffer dams which kept out the waters of the Tweed. Piles were sunk into the river bed or the soft material at the side of the river at 4 ft intervals using a steam-powered portable pile-driver built by Nasmyths. This engine was moved along lines of temporary rails. A platform, or 'floor', was then formed around the piles and the stonework was built up from this. Some of the piles were driven as far as 50 ft into the river bed to ensure stability.

Dressed stone, rubble, bricks, lime and other materials were transported by rail along the approach embankment from the contractor's yard and onto the bridge as construction progressed. Various references refer to the lines as 'bogieways' or 'wagonways'. Records show that, in the early stages at least and perhaps whilst the embankment was consolidating, horses were used to haul the wagonloads of stone towards the bridge with labourers providing propulsion for some of the smaller wagons containing bricks at the yard. Travelling cranes, on craneways, were used on the bridge to lift and lower the stone and other materials for the construction of successive piers. Unfortunately there were several fatalities during the construction of the two bridges involving both local men and workmen from Scotland. Some of these occurred when men fell from the bridges; at least one occurred at the yard when an unsafe practice resulted in a man being killed by falling stone.

The viaduct is 2,160 ft in length and has 28 arches up to 128 ft in height. The bridge was largely built of stone with the underside of the arches being formed from bricks laid in cement. Each pier had an ashlar facing with a heart of well-grouted rubble. The total cost of the contract was about £207,000 of which the main viaduct (sometimes referred to as 'the bridge') cost £120,000.

Four locomotives are known to have been used by the contractor on their standard gauge lines during the construction works. These were all originally built by R. & W. Hawthorn & Co. of Newcastle-upon-Tyne. Two were obtained new, these being inside-cylindered 0-6-0s, *Northumberland* (Works No. RWH 634/1848), and *Durham* (RWH 506/1847). The other two were inside-cylindered 0-4-2 locomotives and were brought north from a contract which the same contractor had completed at Belford, Northumberland. They were called *Ballintine* (RWH 355/1842) and *Cumberland* (RWH 418/1846).

The Berwick contract was completed in 1850 and the Royal Border Bridge was opened by Queen Victoria and Prince Albert on 29th August of that year. The timber viaduct was demolished once the stone structure was opened, at which time a realignment of the main lines at both ends of the bridge had been necessary.

The magnificent Royal Border Bridge carries heavy electric and diesel-hauled trains high above the River Tweed. The contractor, McKay & Blackstock employed both standard and narrow gauge lines for moving materials during its construction.   *Author*

After the completion of the work the contractor's locomotives were disposed of. The first three were auctioned on 21st June, 1850 whilst the last was sold prior to the auction. At the end of June 1850, RWH 506 and RWH 634 went to the Monkland Railways in Lanarkshire, where they became Nos. 23 *Tempest* and 24 *Cyclone* respectively. RWH 355 went to J. Anderson for a Perth & Dundee Railway maintenance contract in Fife. RWH 418, which had left the Berwick area before the auction, turned up to be auctioned by James Hoggins at the railway goods warehouse, Gateshead, on 27th March, 1852. It was said at this time to have 4 ft 6 in. wheels. It was not sold in the auction for it was then offered for sale by private treaty in the following month. Its subsequent fate is not known.

The Royal Border Bridge, after over 100 years of successful service became a listed building, Grade 1, on 1st August, 1952 and, apart from routine maintenance, did not need a major repair until 1995-96 when the stonework was reinforced using the 'Cintec Anchor System'. The East Coast main line, for which the bridge forms a vital component, is now electrified and it was necessary to attach the supports for the overhead catenary wires to the outside of the bridge masonry. It still carries both heavy freight and passenger trains passing between Scotland and England, though the actual border is at Marshall Meadows a few miles to the north.

It is known that McKay & Blackstock were also involved at other locations on the Newcastle to Berwick line, in particular near Warkworth during the building of a viaduct, and at Belford. It is not known whether they used a railway during the execution of the first of these contracts, though the possibility exists. Two locomotives were used at Belford.

23 – Meakin & Dean's Alnwick to Coldstream Branch Contractor's Railway

The contractor, George Meakin & J.W. Dean of Hampstead, North London, laid temporary rails during the execution of their contracts to build the Alnwick to Coldstream line for the NER. Prior to their accepting the Alnwick contract they had executed contracts for the London & North Western, Wirral, Highland and Midland railways.

The Alnwick to Coldstream job involved two contracts. Contract No. 1 was for the southern part of the line which involved the construction of extensive cuttings through stone and substantial gradients. Contract No. 2 was for the easier section of the line along the valley of the River Till. The work started in January 1884 using some temporary tracks. However, Meakin died in July 1886 and it was reported in the *Alnwick Gazette* that Dean had stated that he would be unable to complete the contract. Subsequently the NER completed the work with its own labour. The first public train on the line ran on 5th September, 1887 though the Directors and officials of the NER travelled over the whole line on 22nd April in a train of contractor's vehicles!

The contractor is known to have used seven locomotives during the construction of the line, these being from various builders. It is believed that the builders included Beyer, Peacock & Company, Manning, Wardle & Co. Ltd,

Black, Hawthorn & Co., Hudswell, Clarke & Co., and Fox, Walker & Co. Six locomotives carried names: *Frank* (MW 759/1880), *Sambo, Belsize, Wanderer, Hebburn* and *Cornhill* (MW 892/1884) whilst the last carried 'No. 2'. The works numbers of some of the locomotives have not been confirmed. *Belsize* was likely to be BP1829/1878, *Sambo* may have been MW427/1873, *Wanderer* was possibly MW500/1874 whilst 'No. 2' could well have been FW371/1878. At least five of the locomotives are recorded as having worked on the contract for the northern section of the line.

The locomotives were offered for sale on 26th July, 1887, though they were probably unsold on this occasion as they were auctioned, along with steam cranes, derricks, 150 spoil wagons and rails of scrap quality, at Alnwick on 26th and 27th October in the same year.

The records of the Industrial Railway Society indicate that *Sambo* and *Hebburn* were either sold or scrapped. *Frank* passed into the ownership of the MacDuff Harbour Board in Banffshire, Scotland, whilst *Wanderer* was in the ownership of E. Heathcote & Sons at Dove Holes Quarry in Derbyshire by 1891.

Cornhill was an 0-4-0 saddle tank with 8 in. x 12 in. cylinders and, when new, worked on the last year or two of a contract in Yorkshire for contractor J.P. Edwards (of Ripley, Yorkshire) between 1886 and 1889. It had 2 ft 8 in. diameter wheels. (Later, with contractor Walter Scott it received the name *Luli*.) One photograph of this locomotive has been discovered, unfortunately not whilst in Meakin & Dean's ownership.

One of the locomotives used by contractors, Meakins & Dean, when building the Alnwick to Cornhill and Coldstream railway was the small Manning, Wardle saddle tank locomotive with the Works No. 892 which was built in 1884. Whilst working on this contract it bore the name *Cornhill* though later, when owned by another contractor, Walter Scott, it carried the name *Luli* (*as shown here*).   *Beamish Museum Collection*

Belsize later worked for the Sheffield Coal Co. at Birley Collieries in the Shirebrook Valley east of Sheffield whilst 'No. 2' also hauled coal, but stayed in Northumberland, to become the property of the Broomhill Coal Co. in July 1887.

Whilst carrying out this NER contract, Meakin & Dean (described as 'of Glanton') were also involved as contractor for building the Ladykirk and Norham bridge for the Tweed Bridges Trust over the River Tweed between 1885 and 1887. The bridge, an impressive four-arch structure built of stone, survives today as a Grade 2 listed structure.

A second contractor became involved with the Alnwick to Coldstream line in 1967 and 1968 when George H. Campbell & Co. of Glasgow won the contract for the dismantling and track lifting of part of the line. This firm used a standard gauge, 4-wheeled, diesel-mechanical locomotive originally built by F.C. Hibberd & Co. in 1955. It had the Works No. FH 3700.

24 – Sir John Jackson's Seahouses Harbour Contractor's Railway

Between the years of 1887 and early 1889 (approximately) the sounds of a contractor's steam locomotive could be heard at North Sunderland, now Seahouses, harbour (NU 223322). The locomotive was a small standard gauge outside-cylindered 0-4-0 saddle tank, built by the Andrew Barclay Co. at Kilmarnock in Scotland. Its works number was AB185 and it was built in 1877.

The trustees of Lord Crewe's Charity had placed a contract for the construction and improvement of the harbour at North Sunderland with John Jackson of Westminster. Mr Jackson, later to become Sir John, was the proprietor of one of the country's largest civil engineering concerns. An advertisement was placed in the *Newcastle Daily Journal* of 22nd and 26th November, 1884, stating that an application to the Board of Trade was being made both to improve the harbour and to levy dues for fish landed. An Act of Parliament was obtained in 1885 giving the necessary consent. Construction work was in progress from 1886 to 1888 and involved a total expenditure of £31,189 2s. 8d. Some £16,000 was obtained in the form of a loan from the Public Works Loans Board, £13,997 was obtained from the sale of 'consols' (consolidated annuities) whilst the balance was to be taken out of income. The final repayment of the loan was made in 1908.

The Consultant Engineers for the project were Messrs Watt, Sanderson & Montcrieff of Newcastle. The work involved the building of two piers, one on each side of the harbour and involved some blasting of rock. Each pier was faced with concrete (up to 8 ft thick at the base of the piers) and was filled with rubble. Cross walls were built at 35 ft intervals. The piers were 30 ft high at their outer ends. A maximum of 18 ft of water became available to vessels at high water of spring tides and 3 ft at low water. The Barclay locomotive was employed in transporting stone and rubble, brought to Seahouses by barge from Blyth, for use as 'infill' within the concrete shell. After the completion of the Seahouses project it found later employment on the Devonport dockyard contract for Sir John Jackson.

This 2010 photograph of a cold and snowy Seahouses harbour shows, on the right-hand side, one of the piers constructed by Sir John Jackson, the civil engineering contractor, between 1886 and 1888. One small tank locomotive, built by Andrew Barclays at Kilmarnock, Works No. 185/1877, was used on this contract. Unfortunately no photograph of this is contained in the Barclay Archive at Glasgow University and no photographs of the work in progress have been discovered.   *Author*

At the same time as the harbour development some changes took place in the village square. The low curving embankment which had carried the tramway from the limestone quarry towards the kilns was demolished and the site levelled. A map of the site, associated with the rebuilding plans, indicates that it was the intention to demolish the former lime kilns at the harbour. In the event this did not happen.

Jackson's other British works, many involving the use of railways and locomotives, included the building of some docks on the Clyde, the foundations of Tower Bridge in London, Dover harbour, the naval harbour at Devonport,* and much of the Manchester Ship Canal. Abroad Jackson's built docks and railways in such diverse places as South Africa, Bolivia, Iraq and Singapore. His modest North Sunderland contract must have seemed small fry in comparison! Whilst being too late to help the long-defunct lime industry at Seahouses, the improved harbour was to be of benefit to the local fishing fleet, providing better unloading facilities and a place of safety in storms.

---

* For this contract, Sir John Jackson extracted shingle between the villages of Hallsands and Beesands in south Devon which caused the beach level to drop by 12 ft. Although never officially acknowledged, it is considered this eventually led to the destruction of Hallsands, by storm, in 1917. See *Hallsands – A Village Betrayed* by Steve Melia (Forest Publishing).

25 – The Whitaker Brothers Contract for the North Sunderland Railway

A Private Bill for the construction of the North Sunderland Railway between Chathill on the East Coast main line and the village of North Sunderland (Seahouses) was submitted to Parliament and the North Sunderland Railway Act 1892 was eventually signed by Queen Victoria. There followed four years of wrangling, indecision and stop-start happenings in which the contractors Sharpe & Co. (of Leytonstone, Essex), Pearsons, Philips of Brechin, Carlton Hessey & Co., and Mr A Haslett were involved. By the start of October 1896 a start had been made on the work by Haslett. Part of the route had been fenced, some earthworks had been done and a short length of rail had been laid at the Chathill end of the line. However, no work was actually being progressed by Haslett's men!

On 12th October, 1896 the Directors read the specifications and plans drawn up by Whitaker Brothers, the Horsforth, Leeds-based contractor, for the completion of the work. Negotiations with Haslett were ongoing and were not settled until March 1898. Despite this, by early November the construction of the line by Whitakers was well under way. However, even though work had started, the seal was not put upon their construction contract until 13th November, 1896!

During the construction of the line Whitakers used a lightweight Manning, Wardle 'F' class 0-4-0 saddle tank (Works No. MW1074/1888). Whitakers had bought the locomotive new from its makers and used it on several other contracts in the North East before this one. After completion of the North Sunderland Railway contract the locomotive was transferred to the ownership of Joseph Laycock & Co., who used the locomotive at Seghill Colliery in the south of Northumberland. It was the only Seghill Colliery locomotive never to carry a name or number. It was sold or scrapped in about 1916.

After completion of the works and the necessary inspections the North Sunderland line was eventually opened for goods trains on 1st August, 1898 and for passenger trains on 18th December, 1898. The mooted extension towards Seahouses harbour (where a new station had been earlier proposed) was never made. Similarly the planned Bamburgh extension, to have left the branch line just beyond the station limits at Seahouses, was never constructed.

26 – The Reservoir Railways at Fontburn

At the end of the 19th century Tynemouth Corporation was seeking a better water supply, particularly for the 300,000 persons living in the districts of Morpeth, Ashington and Whitley Bay. Newcastle and Gateshead had already considered the valley of the River Font for this purpose. The land belonged to three different landowners: George Trevelyan of Wallington, William Orde of Nunnykirk and the Duke of Northumberland of Alnwick Castle. An Act of Parliament was obtained in August 1898. The works were put out to tender and that of George Lawson, of just over £164,000, was accepted. The work, to the

Tynemouth Corporation Waterworks at Fontburn. Northumberland.

A commercially-produced picture postcard on behalf of the Tynemouth Corporation waterworks shows some narrow gauge wooden bodied tipper wagons employed on the reservoir and waterworks construction contract. In the background is the magnificent Fontburn viaduct on the NBR's Rothbury branch.   *Author's Collection*

This view of the Fontburn water treatment works was taken, in 2009, from the road leading over the Fontburn reservoir dam, close to the photographer's viewpoint in the previous, early 1900s picture. The Fontburn viaduct, now listed, once again forms the backdrop. Fortunately the Northumbrian Water photographic archive pictures are in safe keeping at the works!   *Author*

design of James Mansergh of Westminster, started in October 1901 but proceeded very slowly. The corporation thus terminated the contract with Lawson and completed the work using direct labour. The finishing touches to the job were being applied at the end of 1907 and the start of 1908. The reservoir was full on 16th October, 1908. A temporary village was constructed for the workers and their families to the north-east of the dam. In addition there was a separate mission house, a canteen and several streets of living huts. There was a shop and a school, also houses for a policeman, a schoolteacher and the canteen keeper, as well as various workshops and stables for 19 horses. There was even a Post Office savings bank! At its maximum the population of the village numbered just over 450 of whom 250 were 'non-employees', presumably wives and children of the workers. After the opening of the reservoir some of the village continued in use for the employees at Ewesley Quarry.

The Fontburn Reservoir (NZ048937) dam lies due south of Rothbury, about 15½ miles south-west of Alnwick. The reservoir is about a mile in length and a quarter of a mile wide at its widest point. It receives its water from the Newbiggin and Fallowlees Burns which originally joined to form the River Font. Today it holds some 730 million gallons of water and supplies 5½ million gallons each day. Its area is about 84 acres.

The reservoir was constructed to the west of the NBR's Rothbury branch at the point where it crossed the Font Burn (or River Font) by means of the impressive 12-arched Fontburn viaduct. Much of the stone used in its construction came from the nearby Ewesley Quarry via its mineral line but other stone came in rail wagons from Blaxter Quarry near Elsdon. This was conveyed to Knowesgate station and thence transported via Scots Gap over NBR metals. Some of the lime used was produced at the nearby limeworks, though much cement was brought in by the NBR, as was sand, crushed whinstone and coal. The coal fired the boilers of the cranes, the 8 hp stationary boilers (for powering the Robey stone crushers and the clay pugmill), the two steam navvies (one Ruston, one Whitaker), a steam roller and the locomotives. The steam engines and buildings on the site consumed 250 tons of coal monthly. Clay, for puddling purposes, was obtained from land at the side of the Font Burn.

The first station at Fontburn on the Rothbury branch was called Whitehouse; later it became Fontburn, then Fontburn Halt. The facilities for passengers at the single platform were simple. The station was situated about 6½ miles along the railway line from Scots Gap station and was on a gradient of 1 in 150. A trap point at the Scots Gap end of the station protected the branch from the effects of any wagons 'running away' in the direction of Ewesley. The first siding adjacent to the station was put in for the reservoir construction traffic in 1902. It was located behind the station platform and was gated. It was referred to in official records as the 'Tynemouth Corporation Siding'. Later a set of points gave access to a second siding. As described earlier all of the points leading to sidings at this location were controlled from a ground frame.

A '3-foot' narrow gauge railway system was constructed with three sidings laid parallel to those of the standard gauge. Here transhipment between the wagons of the two gauges occurred. The rails used on the reservoir system

Roadroller *Incubu* crosses the rail tracks at Fontburn on temporarily laid baulks of timber. This vehicle was used during the reservoir construction works at Fontburn in the early 1900s.
Northumbrian Water Archive Collection

Tynemouth Corporation Waterworks Dept owned *Fontburn*, HC 418 of 1894, and it was employed for four years during the construction of Fontburn Reservoir, arriving from the Catcleugh reservoir job (where it was named *Otterburn*) and being sold afterwards to Blaxter Quarry where it became *Ottercops*.
Beamish Museum Collection

Tattoo, KS 852 of 1904, the first of a class of 0-4-2 saddle tanks built by Kerr, Stuart & Co. was photographed immediately after its arrival at Fontburn in 1904; hence its 'ex-works' condition and the 'proud' staff!   *Northumbrian Water Archive Collection*

Tynemouth, HE 759 of 1901, was the third of four possible narrow gauge locomotives to be used at Fontburn, having crossed the Irish Sea after the completion of a reservoir contract for Douglas Corporation in the Isle of Man. Like KS 852 it was sold to John Best & Sons for further use.

Beamish Museum Collection

Tattoo shunts the narrow gauge interchange sidings and depot adjacent to the NBR's branch tracks. The platform of Fontburn Halt and the exchange sidings for the Ewesley Quarry line are just visible on the right in the far distance. *Northumbrian Water Archive Collection*

A photograph of *Fontburn*, in rather careworn condition after years of hard work, provides a contrast to its condition in an earlier photograph! Note the home-made chimney extension and the bucket hung on the boiler, together with the weatherboarding on the cabside to protect the crew during inclement weather! *Beamish Museum Collection*

weighed either 35 or 42 lb. per yard; they were spiked directly to wooden sleepers measuring 5 ft x 8 in. x 5 in. using 4 in. x 1½ in. dog spikes. Lines ran from the exchange sidings (to which up to 640 standard gauge wagons per month brought materials) to the loco shed (located below the reservoir), to the upper platforms of the concrete mixers, to the stone crushers, to the clay fields (alongside the Font Burn), and to the 'earth borrow pit' for the embankment (located to the north of the reservoir). Three locomotives are known to have worked on the line (and have left photographic evidence); one other is 'remembered' by a local resident though photographic evidence has not yet turned up. All of the locomotives arrived during the 'direct labour' period.

The first locomotive was an outside-cylindered 0-4-0 saddle tank with 8 in. x 12 in. cylinders (Works No. HC418/1894). This Hudswell, Clarke-built locomotive had earlier been delivered new to the Newcastle & Gateshead Water Co. for building work on the Catcleugh Reservoir in nearby Redesdale. Here it carried the name *Otterburn*. Its name was changed to *Fontburn* following its move. After about four years of work at Fontburn it was sold and delivered, in November 1908, to Messrs Blaxter at nearby Blaxter Quarry where it was renamed *Ottercops*.

The second locomotive used at Fontburn was a Kerr, Stuart outside-cylindered 0-4-2 saddle tank with 7 in. x 12 in. cylinders named *Tattoo* (Works No. KS 852/1904), the first of its type to be built. It arrived, newly-constructed, from its makers and was in service after May 1904. After its service at Fontburn it was sold, possibly in March 1910 and for the sum of £170, to John Best & Son for use on the Delph Reservoir contract for Bolton Waterworks in Lancashire.

The third locomotive known to have operated at Fontburn was *Tynemouth*, an 0-4-0 saddletank with 7 in. x 10 in. outside cylinders, built by the Hunslet Engine Co. of Leeds (Works No. HE759/1901). It arrived at Fontburn after working on the West Baldwin Reservoir contract in the Isle of Man. It left Douglas on 20th May, 1905. Its name was changed from *Ardwhallan* to *Tynemouth* when it arrived at Fontburn. After its work at Fontburn it was in the ownership of John Best (*see above*) by March 1909 having been sold, also for the sum of £170.

The fourth locomotive, believed to have been used at Fontburn, may not have done much work there as it does not appear in the archive of photographs taken at the site. It was *Rede*, a William Bagnall-built outside-cylindered 0-4-0 saddle tank with 9 in. x 14 in. cylinders (Works No. WB1413/1894). Like *Fontburn* it came to this site from the Catcleugh Reservoir job. By 1906 a spares order for this locomotive was made by J.B. Watson & Sons. It is possible, therefore, that it had been transferred away by this time or, as suggested by the late Harold Bowtell, that Watson was an agent for Tynemouth Corporation. By April 1908 it was at Rannoch Moor in the ownership of contractor Sir John Jackson (during the execution of the Blackwater Reservoir construction contract).

One photograph of the Fontburn site shows a carriage which was presumably used to move personnel around the site. In addition the railway used many wood- and metal-bodied side-tipper wagons. A locomotive shed was in existence by 1905, though this could only hold three of the four locomotives. In addition there was stabling for up to 19 horses, though it appears that only about 16 were working at any one time. The horses were used to move single wagons, or pairs, over the more lightly laid lines. One locomotive is known to have been required to shunt the exchange sidings whilst two were generally employed on other duties, including moving trains of earth from the borrow pit. Wagons on several self-acting inclined planes brought earth down to the lower level for the trains. These inclines had a slope of about 1 in 6 and each cable was wound around a braked drum of 8 ft 6 in. diameter at the upper end. Four sets of 10 narrow gauge 1½ cubic yard tipper wagons and 16 men, (including three in the navvy itself, the locomotive crew, platelayers, bucket men, labourers and a foreman), were allocated for each steam navvy. The site also had a wagon repair shed, smithy, joiner's shop, and fitting shop as well as the locomotive shed.

There were just two fatal accidents on the Fontburn railway system. On 29th June, 1905 a former collier, Thomas Bergen, aged 34, was run over by one of the railway locomotives, whilst on 11th September, 1907 a 26-year-old local man, Rothley-born John Lane, was fatally injured whilst coupling some wagons together.

Work gradually decreased during 1907 as the reservoir neared completion, with some plant and one locomotive being sold towards the end of that year. There was some interchange of traffic with the standard gauge NBR line in 1908 but by October of that year, with the filling of the reservoir, this had ceased. In December of that year it was agreed that all surplus plant should be sold, the last of the locomotives having left by 1910.

It is unfortunate that all of the reservoir works at Fontburn were performed between successive editions of the OS maps. The 1902 map simply shows the two sidings on the east side of the branch (associated with the limeworks) whilst the 1920s map shows the completed reservoir. Behind Fontburn Halt there appears to be just one of the original two sidings which served the reservoir construction works. The LNER map of the same period also shows the single siding, with its fence and gates separating railway from Tynemouth Corporation property. However, a book by Harold Bowtell (see the Bibliography) contains maps which he traced showing the extent of the reservoir railway system.

Today the foundations of the Fontburn Halt platform and the location of the sidings can be identified whilst the nearby forestry boundary follows the original fence line. A country park with visitor centre has been established next to the reservoir. This is signposted and can be accessed by car or on foot from the B6342 Rothbury to Hexham road. It is a popular site for fishing and there are footpaths through the woods around the reservoir. The magnificent stone Fontburn viaduct on the Rothbury branch still stands and can be viewed from the reservoir dam. There is plenty of car parking adjacent to the reservoir where Northumberland Water maintains the visitor facilities.

A website, designed by Fontburn residents, has been created recently and this shows many photographs of the reservoir under construction. Several of these pictures, derived from the Northumbrian Water archives, show railway operations.

Chapter Seven

A Varied Collection
of Other Railways

Inevitably when placing lines into groups of similar function or geographical location one is left with some lines that do not fit conveniently into the chosen categories. The following lines are some of these. They are geographically widely separated and had a diversity of functions.

27 – The Marshall Meadows Seaweed Railway, Berwick-upon-Tweed

In 1926, referring to a tunnel bored through some 240 ft of solid sandstone rock at Marshall Meadows, close to the Scottish border, James Logan Mack wrote (in his book *The Border Line*):

> This curious tunnel was constructed about a hundred years ago to enable seaweed to be transported from the shore to be spread as manure on the adjacent farms. It was laid with rails, the motive power required to haul up the trucks being obtained from a stream, which at a later date was diverted and the tunnel rendered useless for its original purpose.

This was the source that was used by Francis Cowe, in his book on the history of Berwick-upon-Tweed, published in the 1970s and which has since been reprinted.

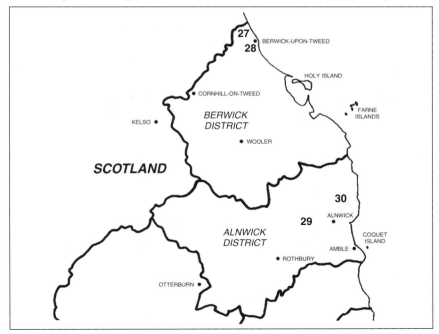

The lower entrance to the Marshall Meadows railway tunnel is simply carved out of the sandstone cliff with no masonry arch or abutments. A flight of steps led to the tunnel from the shore where small boats may have tied up.   *Berwick-upon-Tweed Record Office Collection*

The upper entrance to the Marshall Meadows railway tunnel was located some seven metres below the level of the surrounding ground. This tunnel ran beneath the East Coast main line before partial collapse of the cliffs necessitated it being realigned some 30 metres inland. The tunnel mouth is strengthened with an arch of stone blocks.   *Berwick-upon-Tweed Record Office Collection*

Also dating from the 1920s is a sale document with accompanying plan which was drawn up for the sale of the Marshall Meadows Estate. It contains the following:

> There is also a subterranean passage leading from the Headland down to the bay. Romantic legends are attached to this passage which is said to have been used by smugglers in the olden days.

The plan attached to this sale document was drawn up for Thomas B. Sanderson, the Chartered Surveyor and Auctioneer, of Newcastle-upon-Tyne. It clearly shows the tunnel though its direction is somewhat incorrect. The Plan shows part of the original route of the East Coast main line before its diversion (*see later*) together with the new alignment. The bay below is indicated as a 'private bay'.

Minerals are easily washed out, or leached, from the local shallow soils. Seaweed is a rich source of the minerals potassium, calcium, sodium, iron, magnesium, phosphorus, iodide and chloride and can be used, with care, as a fertiliser or 'manure' to replace the minerals in the soil. There is no doubt that seaweed was a useful, and 'cheap', fertiliser for the local farmers.

However, the question must be posed: in the 1800s would local farmers have bored a huge 80 yard tunnel through solid rock, have laid a railway, machinery and a water-powered winch just to bring seaweed to the top of the cliff? Firstly, a nearby horse-gin (a winding device) already existed for the haulage of materials from the beach to the clifftop and secondly, there were local cart tracks and roads (including the Great North Road) which could have linked the nearby farms with equally accessible sources of seaweed.

The tunnel (NU981567), described by Mack as 'a modern wonder' is carved out of the red sandstone and runs approximately north-south. It is between two and three metres in width (widening to a chamber at the upper end) and, in places, at least two metres in height. In the chamber at the upper end the roof is much higher and is supported by arches made of sandstone blocks. It contains a large space which may have been the site of haulage machinery. Recesses in the wall indicate the possible former existence of timbers to support an elevated floor. The tunnel slopes steeply at an angle of about 1 in 4. It starts in a hollow, some seven metres or so below the level of the surrounding land and emerges from the cliff, not on the shore itself, but some 13 metres above it. (It is a fact that parts of the cliffs have collapsed in this vicinity and the opening may have formerly been nearer to sea level.) From the opening a slope led down to a pier or jetty. (Mack described this as 'disused' in 1926. However, Sanderson's plan, surveyed in the early 1920s, makes no indication of there being a jetty here.). In Mack's day the slope was a grassy one. Today a relatively recently-constructed flight of steps leads down to the site of the jetty, which has now entirely disappeared. Above the top entrance to the tunnel there is a similar steep flight of steps, constructed from wooden frames, infilled with crushed stone. The stepped path reaches ground level at the side of a roadway which leads through a caravan park. The surrounding 'hollow' is partly walled at tunnel entrance level. At ground level a post and rail fence provides some security though there is unrestricted access to the steps via a gap between two large wooden posts. The remains of a lightweight iron mesh, formerly used to block the upper tunnel entrance, stand upright by the tunnel but are in a very rusty state.

Formerly the tunnel ran beneath the East Coast main line, its upper opening being located to the west of this railway. Following the instability and collapse of parts of the local cliffs in the late 19th century, the main line was eventually diverted some 30 yards to the west, away from the cliff edge. The plans for this were drawn up by the North British Railway in 1920 and the work was completed soon afterwards. Thus today the tunnel entrance lies to the east of the main line.

Mack dates the construction of the tunnel approximately to the mid-1820s. However, the detailed plans and sections, drawn up for the NBR and printed in 1839 fail to indicate the existence of the tunnel, even on an enlarged inset of the area. The tunnel is more likely, therefore, to date from the period between 1840 and the First Edition OS maps of the area, surveyed in the 1860s. These maps indicate the existence of the tunnel and the jetty, but no mention is made of any railway, even though a few yards at the lower end, and perhaps the upper end also, would have been in the open air.

For what purpose was the tunnel constructed? A recent television programme featured the tunnel as a route, to and from the shore, for local fishermen. Salmon have certainly been caught in large quantities in the bay beneath the tunnel, and boats, landing other fish, could have used the jetty. No mention was made in this programme of either the railway or the movement of seaweed! Certainly the substantial quantities of fish, especially the lucrative salmon harvest, would have generated more finance for the local economy than seaweed and may have justified the building of the tunnel. Mr Cowe, who included references to both the seaweed and the salmon fishery in his book, has told me in a private communication that a friend of his maintained that sandstone, quarried from the cliffs, could also have been moved through the tunnel. The stories relating the building of the tunnel to the activities of smugglers can probably be discounted!

What is difficult to comprehend is that the nearby stream, or 'burn' in local parlance, was used to power a haulage device. It ran some 30 feet at its nearest point (using calculations based on the dimensions on the NBR plans) *below* the level of the upper tunnel entrance. A long leat, of which there is no evidence, would have been needed to tap the burn at a higher point to provide the head of water needed to drive any haulage engine. It is also difficult to understand why the upper entrance to the tunnel is nearly seven metres below the surrounding ground surface. There is no present-day evidence that there was once a continuation of the tunnel's incline up to the surface level, though Sanderson's map could be interpreted as showing a less steep gradient running northwards from the tunnel mouth. This is, however, in almost the opposite direction to which the tunnel emerges on this map! Today an old-looking stone wall also necessitates a near-reversal of the direction of the present-day path half way up from the tunnel mouth. It is also puzzling as to why the haulage machinery should have been located *inside* the tunnel, necessitating an alternative means of haulage for the final yards to the surface!

At present the tunnel is usually damp as a result of seepage from the ground around the hollow above the entrance. Much sandy soil has been washed into the tunnel and evidence of any track or fixings could only be confirmed by a careful excavation of its floor. Secondary sources thus remain as the only 'evidence' of the existence of the railway here. Further evidence is needed before it can be verified that this was the most northerly industrial railway in England. Until this evidence is obtained the Dewar's warehouse railway (q.v.) can claim this distinction.

The tunnel, at the present time, is found on land belonging to the proprietors of the surrounding caravan park. The approach road is private and there is no public parking on the site or nearby. Permission must be sought to visit the site and the tunnel. Extreme care should be taken when entering the tunnel itself which is very slippery especially after rain. The approach steps are also quite dangerous as some of the stone infill has been eroded leaving protruding wooden kerbs.

28 – The Dewar's Warehouse Granary Railway, Berwick-upon-Tweed

This is one of the shortest of the 'minor railways' found in the north of Northumberland. It is also, if the Marshall Meadows line did not exist, the most northerly industrial railway in England.

For a long time grain has been produced in large quantities on the farms of the coastal fringes of both Northumberland and the Scottish Border region.

The large granary, on Dewar's Lane, Berwick (NU998526), was built in the third quarter of the 18th century, not far from the quay on the east bank of the River Tweed. The wooden-framed warehouse carries the name of a Mr Dewar who was an early 19th century corn merchant in the town. Grain was stored here before being exported by sea-going vessels. Some of the sacks of grain were brought directly from farms to the granary on farm carts. They arrived at the goods entrance on the east side located on Dewar's Lane. Here there was a sack hoist which could raise the loaded sacks from the ground as high as the fourth floor level. 'Taking-in doors' allowed the sacks to be manhandled into the warehouse where they were stored on several floors. Guide rails on the walls protected both the walls and the sacks as they were raised upwards. Other consignments of grain are believed to have arrived by horse-drawn cart, having been transhipped from small coastal vessels at Tweedmouth. This procedure necessitated the loads being transported over the Tweed Bridge by cart, arriving at the granary via Bridge Street.

At some time in the mid-19th century an arch was cut through the wall of the town just to the south west of the granary. A short narrow gauge railway was laid linking the quayside and the granary's west wall where there was a 'passing loop'. Sacks of grain could be loaded from the west door of the granary onto small wagons which were then propelled by manpower along the line of railway to the waiting vessels at the quayside. No evidence of the type of wagon employed has survived, though it is likely that they were of wooden construction with a flat bed for carrying the sacks. The passing loop would indicate the use of several wagons on the line.

During successive rebuildings and 'improvements' of the quay area the lines on the quayside have disappeared and it has not proved possible to identify the

The remains of the Dewar's Lane Warehouse Railway, consisting of a loop and line leading towards the gate onto the Berwick Quay, are seen on this photograph of the building's north-west face shortly before rebuilding and restoration works commenced.
Courtesy of John Smithson, Berwick-upon-Tweed Preservation Trust

John Smithson of Berwick Civic Trust and the author examine the pointwork on the line of the Dewar's Lane Warehouse Railway. After completion of the restoration work the remains of the railway will be preserved and an explanation of its significance will indicated on an information board mounted nearby.

The Irving Gallery for the Berwick-upon-Tweed Preservation Trust

Berwick quayside can be seen taken from a vantage point above the Old Berwick Bridge. The doorway through which wagons on Dewar's Warehouse Railway would have passed can be seen in the city walls between some vehicles on the quay. Unfortunately successive rebuilds have eliminated all traces of rails on the quay itself.   *Author's Collection*

full extent of the former rail system there. A large concrete buttress to support the granary walls was, at some time, constructed just beyond the landward end of the rail loop and this may have shortened the line. Until 2009 an old studded wooden door in the town wall blocked the arch through which the railway formerly passed. The sill beneath this door still revealed sections of the original rail. The door itself was damaged and it was possible, by peering through one of the gaps in the planking, to discern a short length of track still *in situ* within the small granary yard. Other loose rails lay nearby. The gauge of the track was measured as 18 in. The granary was private property and for some years the studded door was kept locked so that further 'casual' explorations were not possible.

The granary was linked with the grain trade for some 200 years until it was finally vacated by a firm of seed and grain merchants in the 1980s. Fortunately it is now a Grade II listed building. A development of the granary under the auspices of the Berwick-upon-Tweed Preservation Trust is now in progress (2009-10). Costing about £5m (much raised from grants and private donations) this extensive project will involve the strengthening of the building with hidden internal steel beams. The building will ultimately house a Bistro with open courtyard, a youth hostel (including facilities for the disabled and kitchen facilities) and office accommodation. A through walkway, open to the public, will be created between the quayside and Bridge Street via the railway arch and the courtyard. The surviving railway tracks, from the passing loop to the arch in the town walls, will be left *in situ*. At the conclusion of the project an interpretative panel will be erected which will describe and explain the history of the granary and its railway.

29 – The Lemmington Hall (Felbridge Monument) Railway, near Alnwick

The Evelyn Column, often referred to as the Felbridge Monument, is located in the grounds of Lemmington Hall (NU124109) to the west-south-west of Alnwick on the north side of the Alnwick to Rothbury road (B6341).

It was originally constructed in 1785 or 1786 in the grounds of Felbridge Place, Surrey. It was commissioned in the autumn of 1785 from John Soane, who became architect to the Bank of England in 1788. Its cost was £280. It was made of stone from Turners Hill in West Sussex. Variously its height has been recorded as '57 feet', '75 feet', '85 feet' and '16 metres approx'! It was erected for the owner of Felbridge Place, James Evelyn, in memory of his parents.

The column was purchased in the mid-1920s by Sir Stephen Aitchison (1863-1942) who decided to move it to Lemmington Hall, Alnwick, which he had bought as a derelict shell in 1913. The monument was dismantled in 1927 and moved to Northumberland by a firm called Diambers of London at a cost of £1,470. The dismantled column was transported north by rail. It has been recorded that the stone was unloaded at Edlingham station and moved '...on a light electric railway' to its Lemmington Hall site. This poses certain problems! For example, the loop at Edlingham station is short and the sidings there were on the 'wrong' side of the line for a small line to be laid direct to Lemmington. The station site is cramped, with the high embankment leading to Edlingham viaduct to the west and a steep-sided cutting to the east. Also the yard at Edlingham had no fixed crane for the transhipment of the stone (though

The Felbridge Monument was removed from Surrey to Northumberland by sea, rail, traction engine and finally a short narrow gauge railway. The snow-covered Cheviot Hills provide the backdrop to this early 2010 picture. The line bringing the stone from the roadside passed close to the photographer's position.   *Author*

admittedly a rail-mounted crane could have been used). Furthermore the station sidings lay just below the 400 ft contour on the old maps. The monument site at Lemmington is just above the 400 ft line; however, the route of just over a mile between the two would have involved several steep gradients, with substantial bridges for the crossing of the streams at Swinhope Letch and Corby's Letch which lie below the 300 ft contour. The terrain here is rough and rocky, hardly conducive to the laying of a light railway without earthworks to produce a suitable trackbed. The remains of any such works cannot be seen. The possible source of the electricity supply is not known. An alternative means of movement of the stones was surely employed.

Fortunately the actual events were recalled and passed to me by an elderly gentleman, a farmer whose family had farmed nearby in the 1920s. His account is very different and more plausible! He states that the train of stone was taken to Whittingham station, the next along the branch from Edlingham. This station site here is level and there were longer sidings for facilitating unloading. The yard possessed a crane and there was easy access to the Whittingham to Alnwick road. The blocks of stone were hauled on a trailer from the station yard by a traction engine. Turning right soon after the Battle bridge, the small road leading past Lemmington Hall was followed as far as a point just below the bridge beneath the (then LNER) Alnwick to Cornhill branch railway. From the roadside, a line of temporary rails was laid. Individual stones were then transferred to a small rail wagon which was lowered down the gentle gradient to the site chosen for the monument, the winch on the back of the engine controlling the speed of the wagon by means of a steel cable. The line was less than 200 yards long and traversed evenly sloping ground. It was only necessary to use the line for a few days. No earthworks were involved and hence no remains of this short-lived line have survived.

30 – The Little Mill Preservation Society's Railway

After the cessation of work at the quarry and limeworks at Little Mill, a group of enthusiasts, based in Alnwick, decided to attempt to create a narrow gauge railway based on this limestone quarry (NU227173). A letter from one of their number, a Mr M. Robson of Alnwick, was written to the Howick Estate on 9th January, 1969 as follows: 'We request permission to continue with the building of a 2 ft gauge line at Little Mill Limeworks'. This strongly suggests that the group already had some rails in place. He went on to state that the group hoped to purchase an engine for the line which would be named *Harry Richardson* after the former limeworks owner. It was the group's intention to have the line open and operating in 1971.

The estate's immediate reply was positive in that the building of the line was allowed to proceed but it was stated that a maximum limit of four persons would be permitted to work on the site at any one time. However, there was a cautionary note. The estate said that the group would not be able to continue with their scheme if the executors of the late Harry Richardson decided that the rails should be sold for scrap. The failure of the scheme may well be attributed to that cause.

Chapter Eight

Proposed Railways

Searches through documents held at record offices and in newspaper archives have revealed several descriptions and plans relating to railways which were proposed but apparently never built. In some cases a start may have been made on their construction or rolling stock may have been purchased. Most were associated with movements of goods or minerals though at least two could have involved carriage of passengers.

31 – Sir Francis Blake's Railway

Sir Francis Blake, Bart., was a local landowner resident at Tillmouth Castle. Amongst the properties that he owned were the farms at Bowsden and Bowsden Moor, reached by minor trackways leading westwards from the Wooler to Berwick road, north of Lowick. On the land of these farms, and others nearby at Greenlawalls (now Greenlaw Walls) were considerable reserves of limestone and coal. It was Blake's wish to exploit the reserves on a commercial basis and to supply these commodities via a railway, firstly to the south side of the Tweed at Coldstream Bridge (today Cornhill), and then later to Kelso in Scotland.

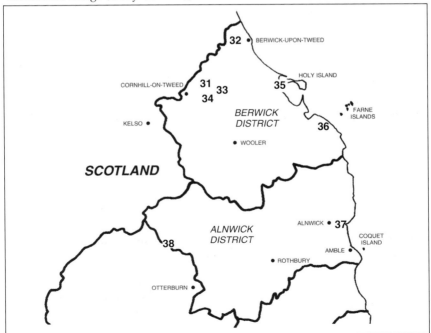

Two advertisements, printed successively, appeared in the *Berwick Gazette and Advertiser* of 27th January, 1811. The first referred to the letting of two farms: Bowsden Farm in the Parish of Lowick with 370 acres of arable land and Bowsden Moor Farm (NT968425) which possessed 436 acres of land. Coal and a limeworks were said to be found on these lands. (There are two limeworks near to Bowsden Farm shown on old maps, and the indication of an 'Engine' near to Bowsden Moor Farm suggests that a colliery was located there.) Below the advertisement for the letting of the farms was an advertisement headed 'To Contractors', also placed by Blake. This advertisement requested estimates from local contractors for the making of an 'Iron Rail Road' from Bowsden Moor to Coldstream Bridge, this distance being quoted as 'Nine Miles'. The contractors would also need to construct a Staith at the terminus for the delivery of coals. Further details of the particulars of the undertaking were available from a certain Mr Darling at Twizell Lodge, to whom the submissions of the final estimates were to be made. The route would have involved crossing Bowsden Moor and the bridging of the River Till, but only a few minor public trackways needed to be crossed before the route approached the River Tweed. A note following the advertisement referred to certain 'conditions' being produced at the time of the letting of the farms, perhaps to allow for the railway and the planned industrial expansion on the land.

Sir Francis clearly had second thoughts about the terminus of his line for in two subsequent editions of the local newspaper, dated 16th February and 23rd February, 1811, he placed new advertisements (actually dated 12th February). The first referred to the construction of an 'Iron Rail *Way*' whilst the second was once again headed 'To Contractors'.

The first advertisement revealed Blake's plans to extend his Bowsden line beyond Coldstream to Kelso, thus shortening the route from this town to the source of the coal and lime, by some 14 miles. Specific reference was made to mines at Bowsden and Greenlawalls (NT 940417). The line's extension was to start from the original planned terminus 'depot' at the south end of Coldstream Bridge. It would cross to, and pass along, the north bank of the Tweed before passing through Coldstream's market place. Then it would be carried over the 'Leet' by means of a bridge before crossing the road and heading to the south west of 'The Hirsel' (later the home of the 1960s Prime Minister Sir Alec Douglas-Home and his family) towards Kelso. The cost was stated to be £12,000 though whether this is for the extension alone is not indicated. The notice for the 'Contractors' requested the submission of estimates for the building of the centres for the bridge over the River Till. The line was to be constructed from the 'mines of coal and lime' as an 'Iron Railway' on 'Stone Supporters' (presumably a reference to stone block sleepers). A staith was still planned for the bank of the Tweed close to Coldstream Bridge. The construction was said to need the use of wood, stone and other materials. Further details could be supplied by a certain Peter Rogers of Twizell Castle and guarantees of satisfactory security would be required for the contractors. It is not known if any made submissions or if the route of the proposed line was surveyed accurately.

Blake must have known of the plans for the nearby Berwick & Kelso Railway and it is surprising therefore that he contemplated the construction of a 'rival' line especially as it involved the construction of a bridge to cross the River Till, a not insubstantial river crossing. In addition, he would have needed, in the absence of any mention of a separate Tweed crossing, to have laid his rails across the Coldstream road bridge, for which the securing of permission may have been difficult. In the event Blake's scheme came to naught, as did the contemporary plans for the Berwick & Kelso line described in the next section. Northumberland coals, and probably lime also, were still being taken by horse-drawn cart to the Border towns, such as Kelso, some 40 years after this scheme died!

32 – *The Berwick & Kelso Railway*

Proposals had been made in 1790 for the linking of Berwick-upon-Tweed and Kelso by means of a canal. Despite nothing having arisen from these proposals there was still considerable interest, on the part of local landowners and businessmen, for a link between the two centres.

A 20 page booklet, entitled *Calculations of the probable benefit to the neighbouring country and to the proprietors of an Iron Railway from Berwick to Kelso, passing by the coalpits and lime works in the North Bishopric of Durham*, was printed at the Kelso Mail Office, in Scotland, in 1809. (At that time and until 1844 some of the northern parts of what is now Northumberland were part of the County of Durham.) The booklet contained calculations that had been made in 1807. For example the cost of cartage by road was considered to be 6¾d. per ton per mile whilst transport by rail was estimated as 4½d. per ton per mile inclusive of any railway duties, wharfage or carriers charges. The forecast length of the line was 24 miles plus two further miles of branches to limekilns and coal pits (for example near to Etal). It was considered that, in addition to these two commodities, traffic would be generated to move corn and 'sundries', stated to include wood, tiles, bricks, slates, iron and other goods. It was estimated that to Berwick alone there would be an annual movement of over 3,500 tons of coal and 4,000 tons of lime. The estimated total costs of constructing the line were stated as follows:

Construction of the railway	£36,768
Building of bridges (including crossing the Tweed)	£15,000
Cost of land and buildings	£ 6,000
Extra charges	£12,000
Total	*£69,768*

Earlier, calculations as to the costs of building the 'line of double railway' had been made by a Mr Thomas, described as 'Steward to Mr Mathew Montagu of Denton, Newcastle', in February 1807. He reckoned that a 'yard of way, two sides', would involve 90 lb. of rails at a cost of 1½d. per lb. The rails would be laid on stone blocks measuring 12 in. x 9 in. x 16 in. at a cost of 2s. 0d. per yard. Additionally there would be the costs associated with 'beating, filling, footways and ballasting' costing 15s. 3d. per yard. The cost of 'cuts, batteries, bridges & gates and gate houses' would amount to £190. A Mr Chapman of Newcastle had no doubt that an easy route for the line could be fixed with a '¼ inch per yard maximum gradient' i.e. 1 in 144. This would allow 6 tons to be pulled by one horse though a maximum wagon weight of three tons, resting on four wheels, would be necessary to achieve this.

In 1809 Mr John Rennie was appointed to survey the line and the survey report was eagerly awaited by the proposers.

In the same year, a letter written by a Martin Dalrymple of Cleland House and dated 22nd March, appeared in the *Kelso Mail* newspaper. It was addressed to the 'Gentlemen of the Counties of Lanark, Peebles, Selkirk, Roxburgh and Berwick' and pointed out the merits of a through railway between the Monkton Canal, at Lanark, Scotland, and the township of Berwick.

Thomas Telford became involved and by April 1810 he had produced a report on the proposed railway between Kelso and Berwick. His recommendation was for a route largely to the north of the River Tweed, i.e. mainly in Scotland except on the approaches to Berwick. Additional comments were submitted in the same Report to the Proposers by William Jessop. He stated that a railway was advisable as the current turnpikes were unequal to their tasks. He dismissed the idea of a canal as there would be water problems at the summit sections. He recommended the use of cast-iron rails. Other comments were made by John Rennie. Later Jessop, in a letter dated 31st March, 1810 commented that earlier estimates had overlooked the need for 'branch rails', that is, crossovers from one line of rails to the other. Also the need for stronger rails at road crossings had not been considered. He also recommended the purchase and installation of small steam engines wherever there were inclined planes. However, his opinions were in broad agreement with the content of Telford's report.

The committee promoting the line met in Edinburgh. A George Robinson was described as 'Agent' for the line. Public meetings, to gauge and encourage support, were arranged for Edinburgh, Glasgow, Berwick, Coldstream (at the 'Black Bull' Hotel), Kelso and Peebles.

By mid-July 1910 an Agreement was reached between the various subscribers to the scheme for the Berwick & Kelso Railway, to run between the 'Port of Berwick and the Town of Kelso'. The capital to be raised was set at £100,000 to be sold as 1,000 shares, each of £100. Messrs Hugh Scott, Thomas Lumley and William Rayley were subscribers and Managers *pro tempore* for the undertaking. John Rennie was to be the Engineer. Bankers, in Berwick and in London, were appointed.

Plans were drawn up for the presentation of a Bill to Parliament. It was entitled 'An Act for making and maintaining a Railway from or near Spittal, in the County of Durham, to Kelso, in the County of Roxburgh; and for erecting and maintaining a Bridge over the River Tweed from the Parish of Norham, in the County of Durham, to the Parish of Coldstream in the County of Roxburgh'. Support for the Bill was sought in letters addressed to various Peers by Sir John Buchanan Riddell, Bart, of St Boswell's in Roxburghshire. The letters were sent to many and various Parliamentary Peers and Gentleman Members, including

His Grace the Duke of Northumberland, the Earl of Percy, Lord St John, the Earl of Romney, the Earl of Egremont, and many others. Much support was expressed in letters sent to Sir John, though, in carefully worded replies, a few pledged to attend the reading of the Bill without necessarily committing support! A prominent local Peer, Earl Grey, stated that he was, in the first instance, neither in favour of, nor against the Bill, but stated that if his friend Sir Francis Blake raised some objections, then he would side with him! The Duke of Northumberland also declined to offer support or take shares in the business, firstly on the grounds that the railway would not be in Northumberland and secondly that he understood that there were 'differences of opinion as to the propriety of the measure'. Lord Percy stated his opposition. In further letters Riddell sought to allay fears, writing one letter to a lady landowner assuring her that the rails would be laid as a safety measure only at the side of highways, that compensation would be paid if necessary and that there would be no encroachment onto various private lands. The examples he quoted were Snook Park and the Estate of a Miss 'Kers' or 'Kerr', (difficult to decipher on the original hand-written letter).

Despite the objections the Act, 51 George III c. cxxxiii, received sufficient support and was duly passed in 1811. It authorized the construction of the line, using iron rails and with horse-haulage, between Berwick and Kelso. The granting of the Royal Assent for the Bill was recorded in the local newspaper of 8th June.

However, various problems were to beset the promoters. Firstly there were insufficient funds raised to build the line and, secondly, there were various legal complications which held up a start on its construction. Such matters were presented to General Meetings of the Subscribers, for example that held at the 'Kings Arms' Hotel in Berwick in January 1815. Eventually the time for start and completion of the works was exceeded. Nothing was done and the scheme to build the line was abandoned in 1827, though there were brief hopes for a revival in 1836. Once again there was insufficient financial support.

Berwick and Kelso were, however, eventually linked by a railway, this time with steam haulage of trains, on a line originally laid with double track. The route, proposed by the Newcastle & Berwick Railway, gained Parliamentary approval in 1849. It ran from Tweedmouth and at Sprouston Junction made an end-on connection with the North British Railway's line from St Boswells via Kelso. The through line was opened in 1851 and carried trains for over 100 years until it was closed to passenger services in June 1964, closure to goods following in 1965.

33 - *The Flodden to Barmoor Railway*

The plans for this railway, which would have originated on the lands of Francis Sitwell, date from 1838. The line was planned to run from the Berwick Road, north east of Barmoor Castle (NU003403 approximately), to 'railway sheds' to be built next to the Wooler to Cornhill Road (NT928362). At the Barmoor end the railway was to fork, the junction being located close to the summit of the line. The more southerly branch was to serve two sidings with loading banks not far from the North Field Lime Works on land then owned by a Mrs Grieve. The more northerly branch would have served the Lowick limestone quarry, in particular to 'railway sheds' not far from Eley Well Limeworks and Dryburn Limeworks. The plans show that the line was to head westwards from Barmoor, passing Barmoor Castle and crossing the Lowick to Ford road near to a small quarry. After the summit junction it would have passed through the trees of 'Weavers' Planting', and crossed the 'Coal Road' from Ford Colliery to the Lowick road south of Ford Hill. It would then have passed 'Old Staples', Freestone Rock, and Coxon's Plantation. There would have been bridges over the Wooler to Ford road and also the River Till. A 90 degree turn in the line after the Till crossing would have allowed the railway to terminate close to, and parallel with the Wooler to Cornhill Road on land belonging to the Marquees of Waterford. This westerly terminus would have been just to the north of the Flodden Brick and Tile Works. The total length of the line would have been 5 miles, 3 furlongs and 132 yards, that is, just short of 5½ miles in length. No details exist of the planned gauge or the mode of construction, though at that time iron rails laid on stone sleeper blocks or wooden sleepers could have been used. The type of motive power did not feature in the plans though horses would have been the most likely. Smithies were conveniently located near to the line.

What were the purposes of the line? Running close to the Ford Colliery it would have provided a useful outlet for its products of the limeworks at the eastern end of the line and the tileworks at the western end. It was considered that up to 70 tons of coal per day could be transported along the line, also quantities of freestone from local quarries. With its branches originating near to various limestone quarries and limeworks at the Barmoor end it would have provided a useful means of distribution of their products towards Ford, Coldstream and Wooler. Finally it could have transported the products of the Flodden brickworks towards Ford and Lowick. However, the plans came to nothing and this line was never constructed.

(In 1858, the York, Newcastle & Berwick Railway clearly thought that the mineral resources of the Barmoor area merited the construction of a railway. This company drew up plans for a line to start from Beal station on its main line and to terminate at Barmoor adjacent to the Wooler and Berwick Turnpike Road, close to where the Lowick and Bowsden townships met. The line was never constructed, and, being a proposal of a 'main line' company the details are beyond the scope of this book.)

The absence of the Flodden to Barmoor line meant that the proprietors of Ford Colliery would need an alternative outlet route for their coal if they were to remain competitive.

34 – The Marquess of Waterford's Railway

Plans exist for the construction of a line of railway from the Ford Colliery (NT955377) to the Wooler to Coldstream Turnpike. The line would have been about '196 chains' (nearly 2½ miles) in length. Maps show that a start may have been made on construction of part of the line but it was never completed.

The detailed plans, dated 7th July, 1852, are entitled, 'Sectional scheme for a Railway from the Marquess of Waterford's Colliery at Ford to near the Wooler to Coldstream turnpike road'. They are signed by a Mr B. Thompson, presumably the surveyor or cartographer.

The line would have commenced at the colliery. It was planned to pass the end of the 'new cottages' at a distance of 14 chains and reach the Wooler-Ford road after 24 chains, entering thence into Western Moor field. Here there would be a self-acting incline with the weight of the descending loaded wagons hauling the empties back up the gradient. The head of the gradient would be at 40 chains (½ mile) from the colliery. The bottom of the inclined plane was to be in White Field at 80 chains. The plans show that the line was then to cross 'Limington Road' (actually Immersion Road) at 102 chains, Bradford Bank at 112 chains, and 'Whitfield Road' (actually Westfield Road) at 160 chains. It would cross Cox Pen Park (168-180 chains) before making a bridge crossing over the River Till (180-182 chains). The end of the line (NT 927363 approximately) would be at the roadside some 196 chains from the colliery, that is 2 miles and 792 yards from its start.

The proposals for building the line included the use of stone block sleepers and iron rails, with broken stone, fine gravel and sand being used for ballast. Any cuttings would be 15 feet wide at their base and sloping outwards. From the colliery to the top of the incline a gradient of 1 in 129 was planned, with the incline itself varying between 1 in 16 and 1 in 19. Below the incline the gradients would vary between 1 in 95 and 1 in 171. Above and below the incline it was planned to use 'animal power' with the incline itself being self-acting, i.e. using the force of gravity. It was considered that horses could manage one wagon of two tons of coal on the upper portion of the line, the horses being transferred down the gradient in low trucks (called 'Dandy Carts' elsewhere). Below the incline it was considered that a horse could pull five wagons in a train. In the reverse direction it was considered that a horse could manage a train of five empties back to the colliery on the upper section. Boys were to be employed to lead and look after the horses.

The gauge for the line was chosen to be 'standard'. The rails were to be flat-bottomed at 36 lb. per yard. Wood keys would hold the rails in chairs, the keys being outside the rails. The chairs would be fixed to the stone sleepers by means of two spikes. The intermediate chairs would weigh 9½ lb. with chairs at rail joints being heavier: 12 lb.

The details of the self-acting plane are well described. From the pit a single track would lead to a point short of the top of the gradient. Here the track would become doubled for 110 feet, with a space of 2 ft between the pairs of rails. This stretch of line was referred to as a 'siding', actually a loop. The track on the incline was to consist of three rails i.e. with a shared middle rail. In the middle of the incline there would be a 'by-pass' (of 155 ft), then double track to the bottom of the incline. The track would then be single for 1,240 ft, followed by a passing loop before a single track continued to the 'Depot' at the roadside terminus. No plans or descriptions survive of the proposed layout of tracks or sidings at either the colliery or the depot ends of the line.

Two alternative plans were proposed for the crossing of the River Till. The first version was dated 20th November, 1851 and showed the river as having a width of 72 ft and a maximum depth of 5 ft. The bridge in this alternative would be built on piles, with two spans sharing central piles located near to midstream. The timbers would be cross-braced. The decking, which would be fenced, was to carry a single track, laid on transverse beams, above the river's flood level. The bridge would have stone sleeper blocks on its approach and would have stone abutments for strength. Provision would be made for a footway at one side of the deck. The second plan was for a bridge with a single span, the piles in the middle of the river being omitted and changes being made to the bridge superstructure.

This well-planned line was never completed. Some cuttings, still shown on modern maps, between Ford Hill Farm and Ford village may have been earthworks associated with start of construction of the proposed railway. Ford Colliery, that it was planned to serve, therefore struggled on in much the same way that it had since the first pits at the site had been opened around the 1690s. It was later known as Ford Moss Colliery when the Moss Pit was sunk in 1883. Its coal seam outcropped at an angle of 20 degrees to the east of Ford Hill Farm and on the shoulder of Black Hill. It had, however, always presented problems with drainage. Its coal was largely destined to be used locally, partly to supply the limekilns on the Ford Estate, and partly for landsale. Some was also used to fire the brick and tile kilns adjacent to the pit. The proposed railway could have opened up new markets.

Records show that sledges were used underground to move the coal to the base of the Ford shaft though one document, dating from 1829, refers to 'coal tups' [sic] and 'tramwood', suggesting that some rail-mounted wagons may have been used. It has been suggested that some of the cart tracks on the surface at the colliery may once have been tramways. A maximum of 100 men was employed at the colliery at any one time, though numbers were usually well below this figure.

The final lease of Ford Colliery was terminated on 1st January, 1919. Just before that time coal was being carted by road to Ford village, to Lowick and to Wooler. After the coming of the main line and branch railways, which brought coal from elsewhere to the surrounding district, the price of coal had declined and it had become difficult for the somewhat isolated Ford Colliery, with its associated transport problems, to compete. The Marquess' Railway, if constructed, may just have tipped the balance more in its favour.

Remains of beam engine houses and a possible winding house, including a chimney (Grade 2 listed), survive at the colliery site though at different times both horse-gins and small 'donkey engines' with winches were used to raise the coal. The whole site is now a Scheduled Monument.

35 – The Holy Island Branch Railway

By 1900 Mr L. Morley Crossman had inherited the 'Lordship of the Manor' title for the Holy Island of Lindisfarne. At that time the limestone industry on the island had ceased and fishing had reverted to being the principal industry. However, the fishermen were hampered in the efforts to sell their produce on the mainland by the lack of decent surface communication with the mainland, the traverse of the sands being dependent on the times and heights of tides.

Crossman was aware that no improvements had been made to the island's harbours for some 40 years and, in 1903, he proposed a new concrete and timber pier at the harbour to stimulate the fishing trade. Together with this he proposed a private standard gauge railway to be built from a point near Goswick station (NU046459) on the main Newcastle to Edinburgh line to link with the proposed new pier (NU134416). His scheme may, perhaps, have been inspired by the construction, further to the south, of the new independent railway linking Chathill and the fishing port of North Sunderland Seahouses.

The proposed branch railway to Holy Island would have involved the construction of a long metal 'pier' to link with the East Coast main line near to Goswick. This drawing depicts what a train crossing the pier might have been like with two coaches and a Manning, Wardle locomotive.   *Peter Westley*

HOWICK,
LESBURY,
NORTHUMBERLAND.

25th Oct. 1903.

Dear Crossman,

I dictated a hurried reply to your
letter on Thursday. You ask for an expression
of my opinion as to whether I think that your
proposal that the N.E.R. should build a railway
to Holy Island, would be entertained by the
Board. At the present moment my opinion is
that the chance of profit is not sufficiently
great to warrant such an expenditure of money
as the line would require.

I am sorry to learn from you that the
Sunderland Harbour has not been a success.

I remain,

Yours Truly

Grey

L. Morley Crossman, Esq
Cheswick House,
Beal, R.S.O.

A letter from Earl Grey to the Lord of
the Manor on Holy Island turns down
the proposal that the North Eastern
Railway should construct a branch to
serve the Island.

Berwick-upon-Tweed Record Office

North Eastern Railway.
General Manager's Office.
York.

9th November 1903.

Dear Sir,

Referring to your letter of the 21st
ultimo asking whether this Company would entertain the
idea of making a railway across the sands to Holy
Island. I am afraid that you will not find
anyone to support your suggestion. One looks on
all proposals which involve expenditure of capital
in order to see whether the expenditure is likely to
be remunerative, and I do not think that a railway to
Holy Island would pay.

I regret therefore that the Company
would not be disposed to entertain the suggestion.

Yours faithfully,

L. Morley Crossman Esq.,
Cheswick House,
Beal, R.S.O.
Northumberland.

A letter from the General Manager's office
of the NER at York pours cold water on
Morley Crossman's proposal for a Holy
Island branch railway from the East Coast
main line at Goswick.

Berwick-upon-Tweed Record Office

Crossman consulted the engineering concern of Vaughan & Dymond, based at the Quayside in Newcastle. Following receipt of Crossman's specifications, plans for the new pier were drawn up to include wooden piers set in concrete, a timber decking, staircase and iron bollards. The approach would be made to include concrete walls and filling strong enough to support the railway. The railway itself was proposed to be carried from the mainland on either a causeway or an elevated pier of about 1½ miles in length at an unspecified cost. An elevated pier was Crossman's preference.

At the same time Crossman, who could clearly not afford to finance both the pier and the railway himself, was in touch with both Mr Gibb, the General Manager of the NER based at York, and Earl Grey, the local landowner who was a Director of the same company, as regards the construction and operation of the branch. Gibb's reply was most discouraging:

> … you will not find anyone to support your suggestion. One looks at all proposals which involve expenditure of capital in order to see whether the expenditure is likely to be remunerative and I do not think that a railway to Holy Island would pay.

Earl Grey's reply was, not surprisingly, equally discouraging and the proposals were shelved forever!

36 – The Seahouses Miniature Railway

An edition of the *Berwick Advertiser* newspaper reported briefly, in 1965, that plans had been drawn up for the construction of a miniature railway near to the seafront at Seahouses on the Northumberland coast. None of the local residents or shopkeepers spoken to remember the railway being constructed or operated and it appears that nothing came of this scheme.

37 – The Aln Valley Railway

The Aln Valley Railway Society (AVRS), supported by the Aln Valley Railway Trust, was set up in the mid-1990s with the express aim of reinstating the former Alnmouth to Alnwick branch, thus forming a 'Link from Coast to Castle'. Initial optimism was frustrated, at the start of the 21st century, by the failure of a Heritage Lottery Grant Application but since that time a committee and volunteers have been working hard to ensure that the scheme is successful. A study conducted by Manchester Metropolitan University confirmed the feasibility and likely financial viability of the restored line. A planning proposal by some residents of Lesbury, to turn the trackbed into a public footpath, was successfully overcome following an expensive Public Enquiry and talks with SUSTRANS are ongoing regarding the establishment of a cycle way and path alongside the reinstated railway.

A storage base and work area has been established at the former Longhoughton goods yard (NU240149) at the side of the East Coast main line. Here there are two former German Railways class '323', Gmeinder-built, four-wheeled Köf diesel

Some of the stock for use on the Aln Valley Railway is in store, or under repair, at the yard of Michael Fairnington, Agricultural Engineer, at Wooler, including 0-4-0ST HL 3799/1935 *Penicuick* (owned by AVRS member Chris Donald) and a former BR 12T VEA van obtained from British Nuclear Fuels at Drax. The latter, after refurbishment and a repaint will be used as a stores and tool van. *Brian Cunningham/AVR*

Several Permaquip maintenance trolley vehicles including HCT022, DX98702/6 and 7 are owned by Northumbria Rail but destined for use on the Aln Valley line. Originally in store at Wooler (as seen here) they have now been moved to Longhoughton yard. At the rear of the photograph is a Ruston 200E diesel shunter, also owned by Northumbria Rail. *Dave Shell*

shunting locomotives which found their way to Northumberland via Balfour Beatty and their Channel Tunnel construction contract. They are now in the ownership of Northumbria Rail and until December 2008 were in store 'at Wooler. Their works numbers are 4861/1955 and 4991/1956. Another recent arrival is an ALCO 660 hp Bo-Bo switcher No. 801 (Works No. 77120/1949) which was exported from the United States and worked at Margam steelworks in South Wales until 1983. Other small diesel locomotives, several Mark 'I' and Mark 'II' coaches, Permaquip vehicles and rolling stock items, including a rail-mounted crane, have been purchased, transferred here and worked upon. Track and signalling materials, temporary building accommodation and tools are being accumulated here also.

Other items are in temporary store at the engineering yard and workshops of agricultural engineer Michael Fairnington, at Wooler. These include the steam locomotive *Penicuick* (HL3799/1935) which is an 0-4-0 saddle tank with outside cylinders, owned by the scheme's supporter, Chris Donald, and a Drewry 0-6-0 diesel shunter obtained from Drax, along with a box van and bogie flat wagon. Two unusual flat wagons formerly stored here, now at Longhoughton, were obtained from the Ministry of Defence at Otterburn. It is hoped that a Hudswell, Clarke tank locomotive of Michael Fairnington's, currently being rebuilt at Wooler, can be used on the new line.

Two diesel locomotives destined for use on the Aln Valley Railway are shown at Wooler. On the left is a small Ruston whilst on the right is the Drewry diesel donated to the railway by Drax power station. It is soon to be named *Drax*. *Brian Cunningham/AVR*

Northumbria Rail also owns a pair of former DB Köf shunting locomotives, numbered 50 and 51, which were formerly used by Balfour Beatty on their Channel Tunnel contract. Both have now been relocated from Wooler (where this photograph was taken), to Longhoughton yard. They will find use on tracklaying and engineering trains. *Author*

Michael Fairnington's side-tank locomotive *Richborough* is steam-tested at Wooler; this locomotive may ultimately work on the Aln Valley Railway. To the right the Aln Valley's own Drewry 0-6-0 diesel shunter, recently acquired from British Nuclear Fuels at Drax, awaits works attention. *Brian Cunningham*

Having also arrived from Drax a bogie flat wagon, with a load of track panels, rests on a short length of track adjacent to the works of Michael Fairnington at Wooler.

Brian Cunningham/AVR

Following feasibility, traffic and environmental surveys, extensive talks have taken place between Northumberland Estates (the current owners of most of the trackbed), the County Council, other relevant bodies and officers of the society. The outcome was the planning application, submitted in December 2009 for the reconstruction of the first part of the line. The society's initial aim is to construct the railway between a new station, to be called 'Alnwick (Lionheart)', which will be built in Lloyd's Field adjacent to Lionheart Industrial Estate (NU201121) on the outskirts of Alnwick. A curve will allow trains to access the alignment of the former trackbed initially reaching a temporary terminus near Greenrigg Bridge (NU216115). This section of the former branch line will involve the track crossing the impressive stone-built Cawledge viaduct. Eventually the line will be extended to a platform (approximately NU227114) near to Alnmouth for Alnwick station on the East Coast main line. The scheme will also involve a footpath and cycle way, laid adjacent to the railway line, with separate access from the A1068 Alnwick to Alnmouth road.

Phase 1 of the planning application received the go-ahead from the County Planning Committeee on 1st July, 2010 for the building of Lionheart station and the reinstatement of the track as far as Greenrigg Bridge. Hopefully this 'proposed railway' will soon be able to be removed from this chapter and added to the chapter dealing with passenger-carrying railways.

Two former NATO flat wagons were donated by the Ministry of Defence to the Aln Valley Railway after proposed use on a standard gauge target railway at Otterburn, near to the Bellshiel demolition range. One is now at Longhoughton Yard whilst the other remains at Michael Fairnington's yard at Wooler where it will be used as the basis for a replica of a former NER brake van.   *Author*

38 – *The Military Railway at Bellshiel, Otterburn*

In the 1990s some 60 ft panels of wooden-sleepered standard gauge track were moved to a site adjacent to the Bellshiel Demolition Range on the MOD land at Otterburn. In addition two 4-wheeled flat wagons arrived. These wagons, fitted with a timber decking, were unusual in that they had seen previous service with the MOD in Germany. The nature of the planned railway has not been discovered though it has been suggested that it was to have been a gravity-worked target line. However in the early years of the 21st century the wagons and rails were offered to the Aln Valley Railway. The wagons were moved on a low-loader to a safe store at Wooler but the rails had 'disappeared' by the time the railway arrived to collect them!

Acknowledgements

I would like to acknowledge with much gratitude the assistance provided by the following 'official' organizations, individuals and companies that have been very patient and generous in responding to requests for assistance with my research:

Northumberland Record Office at Woodhorn (formerly at Gosforth and Morpeth), Berwick-upon-Tweed Record Office (Linda Bankier and Carole Pringle), Durham Record Office, Tyne & Wear Archives Service, Somerset Record Office, Powys County Archives, Northumberland County Libraries at Berwick-upon-Tweed, Morpeth and Alnwick, City of Dundee Library, British Library (Map Library and Newspaper Library, Colindale), the National Archives at Kew, the Parliamentary Archive, Dundee City Archive, Tweeddale Press Group (*Berwick Advertiser*), *Northumberland Gazette*, *The Times*, Lloyds Register of Shipping, Berwick-upon-Tweed Civic Society, Berwick-upon-Tweed Preservation Trust (John Smithson), the Ordnance Survey, Durham Mining Museum, Industrial Railway Society (Dave Holroyde), Industrial Locomotive Society (Russell Wear and Allan C. Baker), the Historical Model Railway Society (Peter Swift), North of England Open Air Museum at Beamish, National Railway Museum Library, Companies House, Narrow Gauge Railway Society (Clive Walters), the Ruston Archive (Ray Hooley), Devon Railway Centre, Fife Family History Society, Scottish Stone Liaison Group, Smiths Gore (James Boulton), Plateway Press, Forestry Commission (Kielder District), Australian War Memorial Research Centre, National Railway Museum (C.P. Atkins), Department of Veterans Affairs in Canberra, Australia (Richard Reid), Royal Artillery Museum (Matthew Buck and Paul Evans), Berwick-upon-Tweed Museum, Wooler Information Centre, Glendale Gateway Trust, Northumberland County Council Conservation Team, Alan Keef Ltd, Northumberland National Park Authority, Northumbrian Water, Newcastle Local Studies Centre, Defence Estates, Ministry of Defence (Chris Livsey), Public Monument and Sculpture Association, Directorate of History and Heritage of the Canadian Department of National Defence, National Library of Canada and National Archives of Canada, Northumbria Rail, Aln Valley Railway Society (Vera Mallon, Gavin Head, Ken Middlemist and William Stafford), Road Roller Association, the Geological Society of London, British Geological Survey, Building Research Establishment, the Lagan Group, TARMAC Ltd, Hanson UK (David Weeks), Stirling Stone Group, LH Group Services (Henry Noon), Howick Estates, Northumberland Estates, Wallington Estates, Joicey Estates, Lilburn Estates Farming Partnership, Chillingham Castle (Sir Humphrey Wakefield), George F. White (Land Agents), Bailiffgate Museum in Alnwick (Gemma Taylor), the Thorneycroft Register (Alan Sleight), Whitstable Museum (Craig Bowen), Railsearch Images (Thomas Carrick), The Irving Gallery, the Road Locomotive Society, the Royal Forestry Society, the National Trust (Harry Beamish), Leather Family Archives (Michael Greene), Belford Local History Society (Fiona Renner-Thompson), Taylor Wimpey, Bamburgh Golf Club (the late Gordon McKeag), Glasgow University Archive Services, Derbyshire Local Studies Library, and the Mitchell Library in Glasgow.

I have made use of the website of the Durham Mining Museum, the 'keystothepast' website of the Northumberland and Durham County Councils, and the 'Northumberland Communities' website of the Northumberland Archive Service. The website 'Access to Archives' (a2a) has been invaluable in enabling me to identify and locate a huge variety of documents. The internet, generally, has been a valuable research tool allowing me to access records, for example in Canada and Australia, which I would not otherwise have discovered. I have used census records available both on CD-ROM and on-line.

The records of the Industrial Railway Society, the Industrial Locomotive Society and the Narrow Gauge Railway Society have been invaluable in providing me with details of the various locomotives mentioned in the text. In return I have been pleased to pass on to them details which have not previously been in their records, or corrections arising out of my research. In particular I offer my grateful thanks to Dave Holroyde of the IRS and NGRS who kindly read through the manuscript, offered much helpful advice and corrected locomotive and other details.

In a recently published book on railways, an author apologized for not including the names of all of the '101 private individuals' who had provided assistance with his book. I would like to offer my grateful thanks to the 202 individuals (at least!) who have found the time to provide help during my eight years of research. Your assistance, your letters, your emails and your telephone calls have been very much appreciated. Those who have offered photographs will see their name appearing beneath those that have been used. If a photograph has not been used it may well have provided very useful information which I have incorporated into the text. If you have provided me with information, or directed me towards sources of information, I'm sure you will be pleased to recognise the relevant material in the text.

However, it is likely that there will be some errors or omissions. For these I accept full responsibility. I would be delighted to receive any photographs, corrections or additions which would make the descriptions of these minor railways more complete.

Every attempt has been made to identify the copyright owners of the illustrations used. However, some were obtained from unmarked photographic prints or old picture postcards purchased, for example, at postcard fairs. Often these have no means of identification and have thus been described as being from the 'author's collection'. My sincere apologies if your print has been used without permission.

Bibliography

The following books and journals, in whole or in part, contain further reading or photographs related to some of the minor railways and industries in Northern Northumberland; all of these have been consulted.

The North British Railway in Northumberland by G.W.M. Sewell: Merlin Books
Main Line Railways of Northumberland by C.R. Warn: Frank Graham
Waggonways and Early Railways of Northumberland by C.R. Warn: Frank Graham
Rural Branch Lines of Northumberland by C.R. Warn: Frank Graham
Railways of the Northumberland Coalfield by C.R. Warn: Frank Graham
Industrial Railways in Northumberland and County Durham in the Days of Steam by Malcolm Castledine: Book Law Publications
A Regional History of the Railways of Great Britain: Volume IV The North East by Ken Hoole: David & Charles
Railway Stations of the North East by Ken Hoole: David & Charles
Forgotten Railways, North East England by Ken Hoole: David & Charles
Lindisfarne's Limestone Past by Roger C. Jermy: Northumberland Libraries
Lindisfarne Holy Island by Deidre O'Sullivan and Robert Young: English Heritage
Railways in Northumberland by Alan Young: Martin Bairstow Publishing
The Alnwick to Cornhill Railway 1887 to 1953 by Mary H. Brown: The Aln and Breamish Local History Society
The Alnwick and Cornhill Railway by John Addyman and John Mallon: North Eastern Railway Association
Industrial Locomotives of Northumberland: compiled by L.G. Charlton and Colin E. Mountford: Industrial Railway Society (a new edition, compiled and edited by Dave Holroyde, is in preparation)
Lost Railways of Northumberland by Robert Kinghorn: Countryside Books
Industrial Archaeology of North-East England (Volumes 1 & 2) by Frank Atkinson: David & Charles
The Railway Navvies, A history of the men who made the railways by Terry Coleman: Hutchinson Publishing
Dam Builders' Railways from Durham's Dales to the Border by H.D. Bowtell: Plateway Press
The North Sunderland Railway by A. Wright: Oakwood Press
The Rothbury Branch by S.C. Jenkins: Oakwood Press
The Amble Branch by Bartle Rippon: Kestrel Railway Books
The Alnwick Branch by Bartle Rippon: Kestrel Railway Books
Border Country Branch Line Album by Neil Caplan: Ian Allan
Middleton, The Leathers and the Colonel's Railway by Tony Lee: Belford Local History Society
Memories of the LNER in Rural Northumberland by Allan Stobbs: published by the author
The Collieries of Northumberland Vol. 1 by James Tuck: Trade Union Printing Services
Longframlington: A look at the village through photos and stories by John West: published by the author
Wooler to Hexham and Return by Ken Veitch: The John Sinclair Railway Museum, Killingworth
Views of Wooler and Glendale by Derek Fairnington and Roger Mikel: MacLean Press, Wooler
Reflections, The Breamish Valley and Ingram by Sarah Wilson: Northern Heritage
We Can Mind The Time; Memories of Craster People: Ed. Colin Biott: Craster Community Development Trust
A History of Northumberland and Newcastle Upon Tyne by Leslie W. Hepple: Phillimore & Co.
Colliery Engineering: November 1930 Edition
Railway Bylines: various editions: Irwell Press

Various newspapers have been consulted including copies of the *Berwick Advertiser*, the *Northumberland Gazette* and the *Cumberland News*, also trade journals including the *Stone Trade Journal, Contract Journal* and *Machinery Market*.

Bound volumes of the *Berwick Advertiser* are located in the offices of the company which still produces this newspaper in Berwick, though it is probably easier to conduct inspections at Berwick Public Library or at Berwick Record Office where most editions of this newspaper (and others covering the local area) are available on microfilm. It is advisable to book ahead to reserve a microfilm reader at both places.

Bound volumes of the *Northumberland Gazette* (and other early local newspapers which covered the Alnwick area) are held at the Bailiffgate Museum in Alnwick where they can be inspected for a small fee. A few bound volumes, free to view, are kept at Alnwick Public Library. Other editions have been microfilmed and are available for inspection at the same library.

Microfilm copies of Berwick, Alnwick, Carlisle, Gateshead and Newcastle newspapers, also other journals, can be viewed at the Newspaper Library in Colindale, London, though it is essential to make reservations in advance.

The many original documents consulted can be found at various locations, including the Berwick-upon-Tweed Record Office, the Northumberland Record Office at Woodhorn (formerly at Gosforth and Morpeth), the Durham University Archive, the National Archives at Kew, and in other public and private collections (see 'Acknowledgements'). Many of the colliery records, formerly with the Northumberland Record Office, have been moved recently to the North of England Institute of Mining and Mechanical Engineers in Westgate Road, Newcastle-upon-Tyne.

Although the initial work on the Heatherslaw Light Railway's locomotive *Bunty* was performed in Northumberland it was completed by Alan Keef Ltd at Ross-on-Wye in Herefordshire as the works plate, carried by the locomotive, shows.   *Author*